There are many bool  intelligent design. Most of them tend to be tomes that swamp you with information. What makes this clever book unique is the fact that it makes a great argument for intelligent design based on the words, research, and conclusions of secular mathematicians, physicists, biologists, and historians ...(skeptics)... and does so in just over 100 pages. There was one chapter that spent a few paragraphs talking about a concept called "irreducible complexity". This topic was explained in a brilliant and easily understandable manner, and the implications were so stunning that afterwards I laid in bed for hours trying to sleep while my mind raced thinking about it. All sources were clearly referenced, and the sources listed will provide even more reading for me in the future. I have been an avid reader my whole life, and I can say that this is the first book that I have ever finished and immediately started over again at page one. I highly recommend it.

-- *Jeffrey Lyons, Electronics Technician*

1

Wow! A fascinating compilation of well-researched evidence here builds the case for life's incredibly precise design, along with the extreme improbability that it happened by chance.

-- Nancy Chappell, Instructor, Kumon Math and Reading Center of Springfield

Books can be helpful in several ways, one to edify and equip the reader, and another is to be used as a referral to those seeking for answers, a springboard for further conversations. I have found that this book does both. It affirmed and confirmed many of my previous understandings , but it has also helped me in sharing these insights and not having to do the work again and again. Steve's exhaustive bibliography in each chapter really brings things out of hearsay, but plainly states what they did say. I recommend this book to any who are looking for a logical, Biblically based look at our Universe.

-- Pastor David "Waxer" Tipton, PhD

Also by Steve J. Williams:

The Skeptics' Guide to Eternal Bliss

WHAT YOUR ATHEIST PROFESSOR DOESN'T KNOW (BUT SHOULD)

An exploration of the implications of modern
science, archaeology, history and philosophy

Stephen Joseph Williams

Publisher:RFH

<><>

Copyright © 2009, 2010, 2011, 2012, 2013, 2014

Dedicated to my family;

my second favorite puzzle,

whom I also love more than myself.

Many thanks also to Dr. William Lane Craig (www.reasonablefaith.org), the most precise philosopher on earth, who has substantially refined, revised and improved 21st century metaphysics.

Other thinkers to whom I owe a debt include: Dr. J.P Moreland, Greg Koukl (and his team: www.str.org), Dr. Hugh Ross (and his team: www.reasons.org), Dr. Ravi Zacharias, Dr. Francis Schaeffer, Dr. Stephen Meyer, Dr. William Dembski, Dr. Michael Behe and Phil Johnson, Esq. (www.discovery.org). I'm sure I forgot some names, but anybody who is a Truth-seeker on this mortal coil, I thank you.

Some encouragers I'd like to thank for putting some special "wind under my wings" include Jeffrey Lyons, Nancy Chappell and David Tipton.

TABLE OF CONTENTS

FOREWORD

"Collective probability" is the concept I suggest you keep in mind while reading this book. In each chapter we can estimate whether or not the evidence is less than, or greater than, a 50% likelihood for each proposition considered. As the brilliant French thinker Blaise Pascal observed in his famous "wager", if the collective case for Christianity even reaches a roughly 50% likelihood, one should believe in it. The reason for this is that in believing, one has nothing substantial to lose, and everything to gain. Eternity is a lot longer than this life on earth! It is my contention that the evidence is far greater than 50% in each case considered, and the overall case is overwhelming.

Speaking of Frenchmen, a probability theorist from France named Emile Borel calculated what is sometimes called "the threshold of mathematical possibility" in the year 1909. That number is 1 in 10 to the 50th power (in other words, 1 in 100,000,000,000,000,000,000,000,000,000,000,00

0,000,000,000,000,000), so by his reckoning, anything with a probability that is less than that is mathematically impossible. It's important to understand that the way that these "power" numbers (called "orders of magnitude) are expressed, if you raise the exponent (in this case the "50"), the probability is lower. So for example, if the chance of an event is 1 in 10 to the 51st power, that is less likely than 1 in 10 to the 50th power. This concept will come into play in several chapters.

Recent studies show that people with religious beliefs tend to live about eight years longer than atheists, so there is yet another reason to take this question seriously.

INTRODUCTION

"I'm woven in a fantasy, I can't believe the things I
see
The path that I have chosen now has led me to a
wall
And with each passing day I feel a little
more like something dear was lost

It rises now before me, a dark and silent barrier
between,
All I am, and all that I would ever want be
It's just a travesty, towering, marking
off the boundaries my spirit would erase."

~from *The Wall*, by Kansas

A very wise individual once said, "...you will know the truth, and the truth will set you free". Unfortunately though, there is so much information to sort through that trying to face it, digest it all, and address it fairly can feel like facing a giant wall.

There is also a tendency inside all of us to believe things that are comfortable to believe, instead of following the evidence wherever it leads, and accepting whatever that evidence indicates. This tendency in thinking, however, should always be emphatically discouraged. While it might lead to a short-term feeling of comfort, it will ultimately only leave you in a shallow, hollow place.

I have some good news, though, that I've discovered from much study and relentless truth-seeking over many years, which was triggered by several consecutive near-death experiences. I feel the urge to shout this good news from the mountaintops: "REASONABLE SKEPTICISM IS GOOD, AND THE TRUTH IS MERCIFUL!!!" Come with me on a step-by-step look at the incredible, downright cosmic evidence that I have uncovered, which shows that eternal bliss is available to all of us who are willing to look at the evidence honestly and earnestly.

A healthy skepticism though, is essential to engaging any subject with this level of importance. We don't want to believe in something for which there is no evidence simply for the benefits of self-delusion! The key term here is "healthy". Perpetual unreasonable skepticism is a mistake of its own kind, and is likewise to be emphatically avoided by the earnest truth-seeker. The journey we take will use the tools of philosophy (philo ="love", Sophia ="wisdom") -- the "love of wisdom" -- to analyze the evidence from several different angles, and eliminate what is falsifiable. You don't need to be a professional philosopher to do this, you just need to love *truth*.

The reason we refer to philosophy is because it is the bedrock underlying all other thinking disciplines. Philosophy is the home of reason and logic. All sciences, including theology, biology, physics, and astronomy depend on logical reasoning to be conversant with the complexities of each discipline. That's why the acronym PhD stands for the term "Doctor of Philosophy", which is the title achieved by the highest-ranking scholars in each of these fields. You can't get started without philosophy (logic), so that's where we'll start (and, yes, I know that many in each of these fields have drifted a long way from pure logic, but that's a separate issue that I'll comment on later). In each case, we will ask the question, "what is the best conclusion that follows from the evidence?" We will look at a sequential series of arguments, each building upon the whole, and see what the collective evidence suggests.

CHAPTER ONE: THE COSMOLOGICAL ARGUMENTS

Why is There Anything at All, Instead of *Simply Nothing*?

"Nothin' from nothin' leaves nothin'..."

~from *Nothing from Nothing*, by Billy Preston

I find it quite improbable that such order came out of chaos. There has to be some organizing principle. God to me is a mystery but is the explanation for the miracle of existence, why there is something instead of nothing -- Alan Sandage (winner of the Crawford prize in astronomy).

Why does the universe go to all the bother of existing?--Stephen Hawking.

Think about it; if there were no God, why would anything at all exist? There's no necessity for it. One can imagine nothing at all ever existing. Philosophers have wrestled with the puzzle of why there is anything at all since the beginning of recorded history.

The deduction reached by top modern philosophers on this question is that things exist for two reasons: they are either necessary or they were caused. A great thinker named Gottfried Leibniz (the co-discoverer of Calculus) developed the following formulation of this (and if you find this confusing, just skip over it and come back to it later):

1. Everything that exists has an explanation of its existence (either in the necessity of its own nature or in an external cause).

2. If the universe has an explanation of its existence, that explanation is God [what Leibniz seemed to mean by "God", was "a timeless, personal, immaterial being of immense power."]*

3. The universe exists.

Now what follows logically from these three premises?

From 1 and 3 it logically follows that:

4. The universe has an explanation of its existence.

And from 2 and 4 the conclusion logically follows:

5. Therefore, the explanation of the universe's existence is God. (1)

This is called "The Contingency Argument". This is Argument # 1 for a transcendent Creator.

*At first glance, premise # 2 seems to make an ungrounded assertion, but let's examine it more closely, borrowing some words from eminent philosopher William Lane Craig:

> [P]remise 2 is logically equivalent to the typical atheist response to the contingency argument. Two statements are logically equivalent if it is impossible for one to be true and the other one false. They stand or fall together. So what does the atheist almost always say in response to the argument from contingency? The atheist typically asserts the following:

A. If atheism is true, the universe has no explanation of its existence.

This is precisely what the atheist says in response to premise 1. The universe just exists inexplicably. But this is logically equivalent to saying:

B. If the universe has an explanation of its existence, then atheism is not true.

So you can't affirm (A) and deny (B).

But (B) is virtually synonymous with premise 2! So by saying in response to premise 1 that, given atheism, the universe has no explanation, the atheist is implicitly admitting premise 2, that if the universe does have an explanation, then God exists.

Besides that, premise 2 is very plausible in its own right. For think of what the universe is: all of space-time reality, including all matter and energy. It follows that if the universe has a cause of its existence, that cause must be a non-physical, immaterial being beyond space and time. Now there are only two sorts of thing that could fit that description: either an abstract object like a number or else an unembodied mind. But abstract objects can't cause anything. That's part of what it means to be abstract. The number 7, for example, can't cause any effects. So the cause of the existence of the universe must be a transcendent Mind, which is what believers understand God to be.

The argument thus proves the existence of a necessary, uncaused, timeless, spaceless, immaterial, personal Creator of the universe. This is truly mind-blowing!"(Read more: http://www.reasonablefaith.or g/argument-from- contingency#ixzz2hMlA2v9W)

Now, the skeptical mind might ask, "but what if the universe was always here, eternally self-existent...the same way that most people see God as self-existent?" This is a fair question. Let's look at what would be required if this were the case, and the evidence for and against this notion.

If the universe never began to exist, then that means that the number of events in the past history of the universe is infinite. But mathematicians recognize that the idea of an actually infinite collection of things (as opposed to a conceptual infinity) leads to self-contradictions. For example, what is infinity minus infinity? Well, mathematically, you get self-contradictory answers. For example, if you take an infinite number of moments, number them all as moment one, moment two, etc., and subtract all the even-numbered moments, you have an equation where "infinity minus infinity equals infinity". If you then take the same infinity of numbered moments, and subtract only the moments numbered higher than 3, then you have the equation "infinity minus infinity equals 3". If you take the same numbered set of moments and subtract the entire set, you have an equation that says "infinity minus infinity is zero". You can actually get any answer you want for the equation "infinity minus infinity" depending upon how you word the equation! This shows that infinity is just an idea that we can develop in our minds, not something that exists in reality. David Hilbert, perhaps the greatest mathematician of the 20th century states, "The infinite is nowhere to be found in reality. It neither exists in nature nor provides a legitimate basis for rational thought. The role that remains for the infinite to play is solely that of an idea." (2)

But that entails that since past events are not just ideas, but are real, the number of past events must be finite. Therefore, the series of past events within the universe cannot just go back forever, as this would entail "an infinite regress." Rather the universe must have begun to exist.

This conclusion has been confirmed by remarkable discoveries in astronomy and astrophysics. From ancient times, many deep thinkers like Plato and Aristotle assumed that the universe had existed eternally into the past. Of course, the Hebrew and Christian cultures believed in the creation account represented in the Bible, and there were numerous non Judeo-

Christian creation accounts as well, but there were always individuals and groups who thought of the universe as eternal. Subsequent to the so-called "Enlightenment" in Europe in the 18th century (when many in Western Civilization began to drift away from biblical thinking) and even more so subsequent to Charles Darwin's proposal of the Theory of Evolution in 1859, it became very common among scientists and university professors in the West to presume that the universe had existed eternally into the past.

This viewpoint was heavily shaken starting in 1913 when scientists Vesto Slipher, Albert Einstein, and Edwin Hubble discovered very compelling evidence that the universe was expanding. Discovery after discovery in the 20th century affirmed that not only was the universe expanding, but that time, space, matter and energy appeared to have had a beginning in the finite past. In 1965, scientists Arno Penzias and Robert Wilson discovered the remnants of background radiation from the Big Bang. In 1968 and 1970, Stephen Hawking, George Ellis and Roger Penrose published papers that Extended

Einstein's Theory of General Relativity to include measurements of time and space that demonstrated that both had a finite beginning that corresponded to the origins of matter and energy. Remarkably, their conclusion was that (causally) prior to that moment, space and time did not exist!

Latest NASA image of Cosmic Microwave Background radiation

The astrophysical evidence indicates that the universe began to exist in a great explosion called the "Big Bang" about 14 billion years ago. Physical space and time were created in that event, as well as all the matter and energy in the universe. About 11 years of work by cosmologists Arvind Borde, Alan H. Guth, and Alexander Vilenkin culminating in 2003 established that this conclusion holds for all theories of cosmic origin for which there is observational evidence. This is the conclusion of modern science! Therefore, as Cambridge astronomer Fred Hoyle points out, the Big Bang Theory requires the creation of the universe from nothing! That is, from nothing that is physical. This is because, as you go back in time, you reach a point in time at which, in Hoyle's words, the universe was "shrunk down to nothing at all." (3) Thus, what the Big Bang model requires is that the universe began to exist and was created out of nothing physical.

Now this tends to be very awkward for the atheist. For as Anthony Kenny of Oxford University urges, "A proponent of the Big Bang theory, at least if he is an atheist, must believe that the universe came from nothing and by nothing." (4)

But surely that doesn't make sense! Out of nothing, nothing comes. So why does the universe exist instead of just nothing? Where did it come from? Many people think that "nothing" is an empty space, but that's not correct. In "nothing" there's not even space! The best description I've heard of "nothing" (which I think was from Aristotle) is that "nothing is what rocks dream about". Nothing has no time, space, matter or energy whatsoever, because it doesn't exist. We can form an abstract concept of what "nothing" is, but true "nothing" doesn't even have that -- it is truly nothing.

Therefore, there must have been a cause which brought the universe into being. And from the very nature of the case, this cause must be an uncaused, changeless, timeless, and immaterial being which created the universe. It must be uncaused because there cannot be an infinite regress of causes--that is to say, there cannot be a series of causes extending backwards in time to infinity past.

Some Quantum physicists claim that the universe could have arisen uncaused in a "quantum vacuum", but to assert this is to prove Einstein's maxim that "Scientists make lousy philosophers". Scientists are not in agreement that Quantum fluctuations are uncaused, but even if one were to grant this possibility, they only happen in a sea of fluctuating energy with a rich physical structure and subject to physical laws, which far from being nothing, is within space and is undulating with matter and energy.

The cause of the universe then must be timeless and therefore changeless, at least without the universe, because it created time. Because it also created space, it must transcend space as well and therefore be immaterial, not physical.

This brings us to Argument # 2:

The Kalam Cosmological Argument

"You see it's all clear, you were meant to be here,

from the beginning."

~from "*From the Beginning*", by E.L.P.

This argument is deceptively simple, and was used extensively by an 11th century Muslim theologian named Al Ghazali. The word "Kalam" means "speech" in Arabic. In its modern form (as developed by philosopher William Lane Craig) has never been successfully refuted:

Premise 1: Everything that begins to exist has a cause.

Premise 2: The universe began to exist.

Conclusion 1: Therefore, the universe must have a cause. (5)

Regarding premise 1, notice that the classical notion of God would not be included in this category, as He never began to exist within that understanding. From that viewpoint, He is the necessary "Uncaused Cause" of the universe who created time itself, and has always existed timelessly ("eternally"). The universe, on the other hand, is believed by the majority of both secular and Christian scientists to have begun to exist at a finite point (sometimes referred to as "The Big Bang") in the past.

If the Universe Began to Exist, It Must Have a Cause

Isn't it incredible that the Big Bang theory thus fits in with what the Christian theist has always believed: that in the beginning God created the universe? Now think honestly about this; which do you think makes more sense: that the Christian theist is right or that the universe just popped into being, uncaused, out of nothing? I personally don't think this is a hard one.

Ever since indications began to surface early in the 20th century that the universe had a beginning, attempt after attempt has been made to hypothesize an eternal model to avoid the metaphysical implications of that. Some of these attempts are; the Oscillating Model, the Steady-State Model, and the Vacuum Fluctuation Model, and they have all failed. The "Big Bang" models, which all have a beginning in space and time, have grudgingly become accepted by well over 90% of scientists despite their inherent metaphysical implications, due to overwhelming evidential support.

In a series of papers culminating in 2003, Arvind Borde, Alan Guth, and Alexander Vilenkin were able to prove that any universe which is, on average, in a state of cosmic expansion cannot be eternal in the past but must have an absolute beginning. This includes all universe models that honestly assess the available data. Regarding this, Vilenkin states:

It is said that an argument is what convinces reasonable men and a proof is what it takes to convince even an unreasonable man. With the proof now in place, cosmologists can no longer hide behind the possibility of a past-eternal universe. There is no escape, they have to face the problem of a cosmic beginning. (6)

The Sombrero Galaxy - 28 million light years from Earth - was voted best picture taken by the Hubble telescope. The dimensions of the galaxy, officially called M104, are as spectacular as its appearance It has 800 billion suns and is 50,000 light years across.

So now we've established that we have a cause. Moreover, I think that necessarily, it must also be personal. How else could a timeless cause give rise to a temporal (in time) effect like the universe? If the cause were an impersonal set of sufficient conditions, then the cause could never exist without the effect. For example, imagine that all there is a massive sea of hydrogen that existed eternally into the past, and the temperature is cold enough that it is liquid. The effect (the temperature being such that it is liquid) exists co-eternally into the past with the substance.

If the sufficient conditions were timelessly present, then the effect would be timelessly present as well. Yet if the sea of hydrogen suddenly froze 11 billion years ago, we'd have ample cause to wonder why. Likewise, if we grant (for the sake of discussion) the possibility of an eternal past, there is no good reason that the universe wouldn't be co-eternal with its impersonal cause. We certainly shouldn't be seeing evidence that it suddenly burst into existence 13.73 billion years ago for no apparent reason. The only way for the cause to be timeless but for the effect to begin in time is if the cause is a personal agent who freely chooses to create an effect in time without any prior determining conditions. And, thus, we are brought, not merely to the transcendent cause of the universe, but to its personal Creator.

Regarding the age of the universe, many will wonder if this rules out the Biblical description of creation, as most Bible translations state in the book of Genesis that the universe was made in six days. Now, granted, it is possible that God made the universe in six literal days, and built the appearance of old age into it. But notice that the Hebrew word "yom", which is typically translated as "day" in the book of Genesis, can actually also mean "long period of time". In addition, the words "ereb" and "boqer", which are commonly translated as "evening" and "morning", can also mean "ending" and "beginning". Also, according to the fourth chapter of the book of Hebrews in the Bible, we are still in the seventh "yom", so obviously some days are much longer than 24 hours.

The primary focus in the Genesis account is on WHO did the creating, not on the time frame. There are actually 24 other references to creation in the Bible, and they all jibe with long periods of time and an expanding universe. Many interpreters of the Biblical account, including Hebrew scholars such as Onkelos (2nd century), Rashi (1040-1105AD), Maimonides (1135-1204 AD), and Nahmanides (1194-1270 AD), explicitly endorsed the view that the creation days were long periods of time. According to Professor Nathan Aviezer of Bar-Ilan University in Israel, this is consistent with the way early Talmud scholars approached Genesis 1. (7)

Notice from the following table how Moses (who authored the book of Genesis about 3,400 years ago) got the sequential appearance of creature types right! The exact dates are always being quibbled about and adjusted, but it's undeniable that he basically got the sequences right. This was way, way before Paleontology had been invented; where did he get this "inside information"?!

Genesis 1 Creation Days

Creation singularity (~ 13.7 billion)

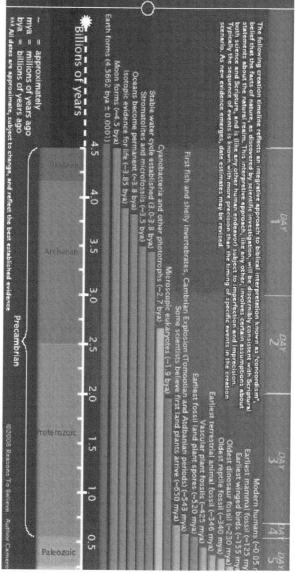

The following creation timeline reflects an integrative approach to biblical interpretation known as "concordism," belief that the facts of nature, as discovered by scientific investigation, will be discernibly consistent with Scriptural statements about the natural realm. This interpretive approach, like any other human endeavor, subject to imperfection and imprecision. Typically the sequence of events is known with more precision than the timing of specific events in the creation scenario. As new evidence emerges, date estimates may be revised.

Billions of years

Earth forms (4.5662 bya ± 0.0001)

Moon forms (~4.5 bya)

Isotopic evidence for life (~3.85 bya)

Oceans become permanent (~3.8 bya)

Stromatolites and microfossils (~3.5 bya)

Stable water cycle established (3.0-3.8 bya)

Cyanobacteria and other phototrophs (~2.7 bya)

Microscopic eukaryotes (~1.9 bya)

First fish and shelly invertebrates; Cambrian Explosion (Tommotian and Atdabanian periods) (~543 mya)

Some scientists believe first land plants arrive (~650 mya)

Earliest fossil land plant spores (~520 mya)

Vascular plant fossils (~425 mya)

Earliest terrestrial animal fossil (~346 mya)

Oldest reptile fossil (~340 mya)

Oldest dinosaur fossil (~230 mya)

Earliest winged birds (~155 mya)

Earliest mammal fossil (~125 mya)

Modern humans (~0.05 ...

Legend

~ = approximately
mya = millions of years ago
bya = billions of years ago
*** All dates are approximate, subject to change, and reflect the best established evidence

Eras

Hadean
Archean
Proterozoic
Paleozoic
Precambrian

Days

DAY 1
DAY 2
DAY 3
DAY 4
DAY 5

©2008 Reasons To Believe, Author Camero

The First Law of Thermodynamics –Conservation of Energy

"Here lies Lester Moore, four slugs from a '44,

no Les, no more"

~epitath on a grave in Tombstone, Arizona

In the Laws of Thermodynamics, we have still more evidence for a transcendent origin of the cosmos. The First Law of Thermodynamics is often called the Law of Conservation of Energy. This law suggests that although energy can be transferred from one system to another in many forms, it cannot be created or destroyed. Thus, the total amount of energy available in the Universe since it came into existence is constant. Matter can be converted into energy, as Albert Einstein observed when he offered his grand equation E=MC2.

Second Law of Thermodynamics - Increased Entropy Over Time

"We work our jobs, collect our pay, believe we're glidin' down the highway when in fact we're slip-sliding away"

~from Slip-Sliding Away, by Paul Simon

The Second Law of Thermodynamics is commonly known as the Law of Increased Entropy. While the quantity of matter/energy remains the same (First Law), the quality or ("usability") of matter/energy deteriorates gradually over time. How so? Usable energy is inevitably used for productivity, growth and repair. In the process, usable energy is converted into unusable energy. For example, heat from pouring a pot of boiling water into the ocean, although not truly "lost", will soon dissipate so that it's undetectable. Likewise "latent" energy, like a wound up spring, will tend toward unwinding (it goes through a "kinetic" stage) and will be dissipated toward "uselessness". Thus, usable energy constantly tends to be irretrievably "lost" in the form of unusable energy. Eventually (absent any supernatural intervention) all matter/energy will reach "maximum entropy"---one might say, a state of maximum "equilibrium".

"Entropy" is defined as a measure of unusable energy within a closed or isolated system (the universe for example). As usable energy decreases and unusable energy increases, "entropy" increases. Entropy is also a gauge of randomness or chaos within a closed system. As usable energy is irretrievably lost, disorganization, randomness and chaos increase.

Since the order in the universe was at its maximum at the beginning, and has been winding down into increasing disorder since then, the question "who organized it initially?" naturally arises. Another thing that we can deduce is that if the universe had existed eternally into the past, it would have long ago decayed into maximum entropy, or disorder. Since it has not, we know that the universe had a beginning.

Another indication that the universe had a beginning is that it is expanding. If you "run the film in reverse" going backwards in time, it all condenses down to the ultra-dense "singularity" from which the Big Bang arose, and prior to that, the only possibility is a transcendent agent which could have caused matter, energy, time and space to come into existence. Who could this entity be?

There are many references to creation in the Bible outside the book of Genesis, and what modern science has discovered matches them as well. For example, take a look at these verses:

Psalm 19:1-2, Psalm 104, Psalm 148:1-6, Isaiah 40:21-22, Isaiah 42:5, Isaiah 45:12, Isaiah 51:13, Jeremiah 10:12, Jeremiah 51:15, Hebrews 1:10-12, and Hebrews 11:3.

These references to such things as a beginning of the universe (that is, of time, space, matter and energy) and to its continual "spreading out" or expansion (it is still expanding today) were not empirically discernible to these authors. They must have had "inside information" to get this right.

The Orion Nebula as photographed by The Hubble Telescope in 2006.
http://commons.wikimedia.org/wiki/File:Orion_Nebula_-_Hubble_2006_mosaic_18000.jpg

Moreover, listen to what some very prominent scientists have said recently, reflecting on the latest discoveries in their fields:

Dr. George Smoot, Particle Physicist, Nobel Prize winner, and team leader from the Lawrence-Berkeley Laboratory, regarding the 1992 observations from COBE (the NASA satellite

Cosmic Background Explorer): "It's like looking at God." (8)

A somewhat more "sober" assessment of the findings was given by Frederick Burnham, a science-historian. He said, "These findings, now available, make the idea that God created the universe a more respectable hypothesis today than at any time in the last 100 years." (9)

Dr. Stephen Hawking (Theoretical Physicist) described the big bang ripples observations as "the scientific discovery of the century, if not all time." (10)

Dr. George Greenstein (Professor of Astronomy at Amherst.): "As we survey all the evidence, the thought insistently arises that some supernatural agency - or, rather, Agency - must be involved. Is it possible that suddenly, without intending to, we have stumbled upon scientific proof of the existence of a Supreme Being? Was it God who stepped in and so providentially crafted the cosmos for our benefit?" (11)

Sir Arthur Eddington (British Astrophysicist): "The idea of a universal mind or Logos would be, I think, a fairly plausible inference from the present state of scientific theory." (12)

Dr. Arno Penzias (Nobel Prize winner in physics, co-discoverer of the microwave background radiation from the Big Bang): "Astronomy leads us to a unique event, a universe which was created out of nothing, one with the very delicate balance needed to provide exactly the conditions required to permit life, and one which has an underlying (one might say 'supernatural') plan." (13)

Sir Roger Penrose (Physicist, Emeritus Rouse Ball Professor of Mathematics at the Mathematical Institute, University of Oxford, and joint developer of the Hawking-Penrose Theorems): "I would say the universe has a purpose. It's not there just somehow by chance." (14)

Dr. Robert Jastrow (Founding director of NASA's Goddard Institute for Space Studies): "For the scientist who has lived by his faith in the power of reason, the story ends like a bad dream. He has scaled the mountains of ignorance; he is about to conquer the highest peak; as he pulls himself over the final rock, he is greeted by a band of theologians who have been sitting there for centuries." (15)

Dr. Frank Tipler (Professor of Math and Physics at Tulane University): "When I began my career as a cosmologist some twenty years ago, I was a convinced atheist. I never in my wildest dreams imagined that one day I would be writing a book purporting to show that the central claims of Judeo-Christian theology are in fact true, that these claims are straightforward deductions of the laws of physics as we now understand them. I have been forced into these conclusions by the inexorable logic of my own special branch of physics." (16). Tipler since has actually converted to Christianity, resulting in his latest book, The Physics Of Christianity.

Dr. Alexander Polyakov (String Theorist, Princeton): "We know that nature is described by the best of all possible mathematics because God created it." (17)

Dr. Edward Milne (British Astrophysicist, former Rouse Ball Professor of Mathematics, Oxford): "As to the cause of the Universe, in context of expansion, that is left for the reader to insert, but our picture is incomplete without Him [God]." (18)

Dr. Arthur L. Schawlow (Professor of Physics at Stanford University, 1981 Nobel Prize in physics): "It seems to me that when confronted with the marvels of life and the universe, one must ask why and not just how. The only possible answers are religious. . . . I find a need for God in the universe and in my own life." (19)

Dr. Wernher von Braun (German-American Pioneer Rocket Scientist) "I find it as difficult to understand a scientist who does not acknowledge the presence of a superior rationality behind the existence of the universe as it is to comprehend a theologian who would deny the advances of science." (20)

Dr. Frank Tipler (Professor of Math and Physics at Tulane University): "From the perspective of the latest physical theories,

Christianity is not a mere religion, but an experimentally testable science." (21)

CHAPTER TWO: THE TELEOLOGICAL (DESIGN) ARGUMENT

"I gaze into the doorway of temptation's angry flame
And every time I pass that way I always hear my name.
Then onward in my journey I come to understand
That every hair is numbered, like every grain of sand."

~ from *Every Grain of Sand*, by Bob Dylan

The appearance that the universe was designed to support life on earth is overwhelming. Secular scientists have observed that for physical life to be possible in the universe, many characteristics must take on specific values, as referenced below. In the secular scientific world, this circumstance of apparent fine-tuning in the universe is not disputed, and is referred to as "The Anthropic Principle".

Atheistic scientists have offered several unconvincing rationalizations for this having occurred without the involvement of a Divine Mind, but given the intricacy of the inter-relationships between various features in the universe, the indication of divine "fine tuning" seems incontrovertible. The list seems to be growing larger and larger as scientists discover more about the universe, but take a look at the list as it stands now. Feel free to skip ahead if you get the gist of it, but doubters asked for detailed evidence, and here it is:

1. Strong nuclear force constant

2. Weak nuclear force constant

3. Gravitational force constant

4. Electromagnetic force constant

5. Ratio of electromagnetic force constant to gravitational force constant

6. Ratio of proton to electron mass

7. Ratio of number of protons to number of electrons

8. Ratio of proton to electron charge

9. Expansion rate of the universe

10. Mass density of the universe

11. Baryon (proton and neutron) density of the universe

12. Space energy or dark energy density of the universe

13. Ratio of space energy density to mass density

14. Entropy level of the universe

15. Velocity of light

16. Age of the universe

17. Uniformity of radiation

18. Homogeneity of the universe

19. Average distance between galaxies

20. Average distance between galaxy clusters

21. Average distance between stars

22. Average size and distribution of galaxy clusters

23. Numbers, sizes, and locations of cosmic voids

24. Electromagnetic fine structure constant

25. Gravitational fine-structure constant

26. Decay rate of protons

27. Ground state energy level for helium-4

28. Carbon-12 to oxygen-16 nuclear energy level ratio

29. Decay rate for beryllium-8

30. Ratio of neutron mass to proton mass

31. Initial excess of nucleons over antinucleons

32. Polarity of the water molecule

33. Epoch for hypernova eruptions

34. Number and type of hypernova eruptions

35. Epoch for supernova eruptions

36. Number and types of supernova eruptions

37. Epoch for white dwarf binaries

38. Density of white dwarf binaries

39. Ratio of exotic matter to ordinary matter

40. Number of effective dimensions in the early universe

41. Number of effective dimensions in the present universe

42. Mass values for the active neutrinos

43. Number of different species of active neutrinos

44. Number of active neutrinos in the universe

45. Mass value for the sterile neutrino

46. Number of sterile neutrinos in the universe

47. Decay rates of exotic mass particles

48. Magnitude of the temperature ripples in cosmic background radiation

49. Size of the relativistic dilation factor

50. Magnitude of the Heisenberg uncertainty

51. Quantity of gas deposited into the deep intergalactic medium by the first supernovae

52. Positive nature of cosmic pressures

53. Positive nature of cosmic energy densities

54. Density of quasars

55. Decay rate of cold dark matter particles

56. Relative abundances of different exotic mass particles

57. Degree to which exotic matter self interacts

58. Epoch at which the first stars (metal-free pop III stars) begin to form

59. Epoch at which the first stars (metal-free pop III stars cease to form

60. Number density of metal-free pop III stars

61. Average mass of metal-free pop III stars

62. Epoch for the formation of the first galaxies

63. Epoch for the formation of the first quasars

64. Amount, rate, and epoch of decay of embedded defects

65. Ratio of warm exotic matter density to cold exotic matter density

66. Ratio of hot exotic matter density to cold exotic matter density

67. Level of quantization of the cosmic spacetime fabric

68. Flatness of universe's geometry

69. Average rate of increase in galaxy sizes

70. Change in average rate of increase in galaxy sizes throughout cosmic history

71. Constancy of dark energy factors

72. Epoch for star formation peak

73. Location of exotic matter relative to ordinary matter

74. Strength of primordial cosmic magnetic field

75. Level of primordial magnetohydrodynamic turbulence

76. Level of charge-parity violation

77. Number of galaxies in the observable universe

78. Polarization level of the cosmic background radiation

79. Date for completion of second reionization event of the universe

80. Date of subsidence of gamma-ray burst production

81. Relative density of intermediate mass stars in the early history of the universe

82. Water's temperature of maximum density

83. Water's heat of fusion

84. Water's heat of vaporization

85. Number density of clumpuscules (dense clouds of cold molecular hydrogen gas) in the universe

86. Average mass of clumpuscules in the universe

87. Location of clumpuscules in the universe

88. Dioxygen's kinetic oxidation rate of organic molecules

89. Level of paramagnetic behavior in dioxygen

90. Density of ultra-dwarf galaxies (or supermassive globular clusters) in the middle-aged universe

91. Degree of space-time warping and twisting by general relativistic factors

92. Percentage of the initial mass function of the universe made up of intermediate mass stars

93. Strength of the cosmic primordial magnetic field (1)

Evidence for the Fine-Tuning of *Our Local Galaxy-Sun-Earth-Moon System* for Life Support

Earth and Moon as photographed by The Galileo spacecraft

http://commons.wikimedia.org/wiki/File:Earth_and_Moon.jpg

Not only is the universe at large apparently fine-tuned to support life, there is an array of features in our more local region of the universe that are also necessary to allow life to survive. The features of a planet, its planetary companions, its moon, its star, and its galaxy must have values falling within narrowly defined ranges (infinitesimally small targets, and all precisely coordinated) for physical life of any kind to exist. (2)

1. galaxy cluster type

    - if too rich: galaxy collisions and mergers would disrupt solar orbit

    - if too sparse: insufficient infusion of gas to sustain star formation for a long enough time

2. galaxy size

    - if too large: infusion of gas and stars would disturb sun's orbit and ignite too many galactic eruptions

- if too small: insufficient infusion of gas to sustain star formation for long enough time

3. galaxy type

    - if too elliptical: star formation would cease before sufficient heavy element build-up for life chemistry

    - if too irregular: radiation exposure on occasion would be too severe and heavy elements for life chemistry would not be available

4. galaxy mass distribution

    - if too much in the central bulge: life-supportable planet will be exposed to too much radiation

    - if too much in the spiral arms: life-supportable planet will be destabliized by the gravity and radiation from adjacent spiral arms

5. galaxy location

- if too close to a rich galaxy cluster: galaxy would be gravitationally disrupted

- if too close to very large galaxy(ies): galaxy would be gravitationally disrupted

- if too far away from dwarf galaxies: insufficient infall of gas and dust to sustain ongoing star formation

6. decay rate of cold dark matter particles

- if too small: too few dwarf spheroidal galaxies will form which prevents star formation from lasting long enough in large galaxies so that life-supportable planets become possible

- if too great: too many dwarf spheroidal galaxies will form which will make the orbits of solar-type stars unstable over long time periods and lead to the generation of deadly radiation episodes

7. hypernovae eruptions

- if too few not enough heavy element ashes present for the formation of rocky planets

- if too many: relative abundances of heavy elements on rocky planets would be inappropriate for life; too many collision events in planetary system

- if too soon: leads to a galaxy evolution history that would disturb the possibility of advanced life; not enough heavy element ashes present for the formation of rocky planets

- if too late: leads to a galaxy evolution history that would disturb the possibility of advanced life; relative abundances of heavy elements on rocky planets would be inappropriate for life; too many collision events in planetary system

8. supernovae eruptions

- if too close: life on the planet would be exterminated by radiation

- if too far: not enough heavy element ashes would exist for the formation of rocky planets

- if too infrequent: not enough heavy element ashes present for the formation of rocky planets

- if too frequent: life on the planet would be exterminated

- if too soon: heavy element ashes would be too dispersed for the formation of rocky planets at an early enough time in cosmic history

- if too late: life on the planet would be exterminated by radiation

9.   white dwarf binaries

- if too few: insufficient flourine would be produced for life chemistry to proceed

- if too many: planetary orbits disrupted by stellar density; life on planet would be exterminated

- if too soon: not enough heavy elements would be made for efficient flourine production

- if too late: flourine would be made too late for incorporation in protoplanet

10. proximity of solar nebula to a supernova eruption

- if farther: insufficient heavy elements for life would be absorbed

- if closer: nebula would be blown apart

11. timing of solar nebula formation relative to supernova eruption

- if earlier: nebula would be blown apart

- if later: nebula would not absorb enough heavy elements

12. number of stars in parent star birth aggregate

- if too few: insufficient input of certain heavy elements into the solar nebula

- if too many: planetary orbits will be too radically disturbed

13. star formation history in parent star vicinity

    - if too much too soon: planetary orbits will be too radically disturbed

14. birth date of the star-planetary system

    - if too early: quantity of heavy elements will be too low for large rocky planets to form

    - if too late: star would not yet have reached stable burning phase; ratio of potassium-40, uranium-235 & 238, and thorium-232 to iron will be too low for long-lived plate tectonics to be sustained on a rocky planet

15. parent star distance from center of galaxy

    - if farther: quantity of heavy elements would be insufficient to make rocky planets; wrong abundances of silicon, sulfur, and magnesium relative to iron for appropriate planet core characteristics

- if closer: galactic radiation would be too great; stellar density would disturb planetary orbits; wrong abundances of silicon, sulfur, and magnesium relative to iron for appropriate planet core characteristics

16. parent star distance from closest spiral arm

- if too large: exposure to harmful radiation from galactic core would be too great

17. z-axis heights of star's orbit

- if more than one: tidal interactions would disrupt planetary orbit of life support planet

- if less than one: heat produced would be insufficient for life

18. quantity of galactic dust

- if too small: star and planet formation rate is inadequate; star and planet formation occurs too late; too much exposure to stellar ultraviolet radiation

- if too large: blocked view of the Galaxy and of objects beyond the Galaxy; star and planet formation occurs too soon and at too high of a rate; too many collisions and orbit perturbations in the Galaxy and in the planetary system

19. number of stars in the planetary system

- if more than one: tidal interactions would disrupt planetary orbit of life support planet

- if less than one: heat produced would be insufficient for life

20. parent star age

- if older: luminosity of star would change too quickly

- if younger: luminosity of star would change too quickly

21. parent star mass

- if greater: luminosity of star would change too quickly; star would burn too rapidly

- if less: range of planet distances for life would be too narrow; tidal forces would disrupt the life planet's rotational period; uv radiation would be inadequate for plants to make sugars and oxygen

22. parent star metallicity

- if too small: insufficient heavy elements for life chemistry would exist

- if too large: radioactivity would be too intense for life; life would be poisoned by heavy element concentrations

23. parent star color

- if redder: photosynthetic response would be insufficient

- if bluer: photosynthetic response would be insufficient

24. galactic tides

   - if too weak: too low of a comet ejection rate from giant planet region

   - if too strong too high of a comet ejection rate from giant planet region

25. H3+ production

   - if too small: simple molecules essential to planet formation and life chemistry will not form

   - if too large: planets will form at wrong time and place for life

26. flux of cosmic ray protons

   - if too small: inadequate cloud formation in planet's troposphere

   - if too large: too much cloud formation in planet's troposphere

27. solar wind

- if too weak: too many cosmic ray protons reach planet's troposphere causing too much cloud formation

- if too strong: too few cosmic ray protons reach planet's troposphere causing too little cloud formation

28. parent star luminosity relative to speciation

- if increases too soon: runaway green house effect would develop

- if increases too late: runaway glaciation would develop

29. surface gravity (escape velocity)

- if stronger: planet's atmosphere would retain too much ammonia and methane

- if weaker: planet's atmosphere would lose too much water

30. distance from parent star

- if farther: planet would be too cool for a stable water cycle

- if closer: planet would be too warm for a stable water cycle

31. inclination of orbit

    - if too great: temperature differences on the planet would be too extreme

32. orbital eccentricity

    - if too great: seasonal temperature differences would be too extreme

33. axial tilt

    - if greater: surface temperature differences would be too great

    - if less: surface temperature differences would be too great

34. rate of change of axial tilt

    - if greater: climatic changes would be too extreme; surface temperature differences would become too extreme

35. rotation period

- if longer: diurnal temperature differences would be too great

- if shorter: atmospheric wind velocities would be too great

36. rate of change in rotation period

- if longer: surface temperature range necessary for life would not be sustained

- if shorter: surface temperature range necessary for life would not be sustained

37. planet age

- if too young: planet would rotate too rapidly

- if too old: planet would rotate too slowly

38. magnetic field

- if stronger: electromagnetic storms would be too severe; too few cosmic ray protons would reach planet's troposphere which would inhibit adequate cloud formation

- if weaker: ozone shield would be inadequately protected from hard stellar and solar radiation

39. thickness of crust

- if thicker: too much oxygen would be transferred from the atmosphere to the crust

- if thinner: volcanic and tectonic activity would be too great

40. albedo (ratio of reflected light to total amount falling on surface)

- if greater: runaway glaciation would develop

- if less: runaway greenhouse effect would develop

41. asteroidal and cometary collision rate

- if greater: too many species would become extinct

- if less: crust would be too depleted of materials essential for life

42. mass of body colliding with primordial Earth

   - if smaller: Earth's atmosphere would be too thick; moon would be too small

   - if greater: Earth's orbit and form would be too greatly disturbed

43. timing of body colliding with primordial Earth

   - if earlier: Earth's atmosphere would be too thick; moon would be too small

   - if later: sun would be too luminous at epoch for advanced life

44. collision location of body colliding with primordial Earth

   - if too close to grazing: insufficient debris to form large moon; inadequate annihilation of Earth's primordial atmosphere; inadequate transfer of heavy elements to Earth

- if too close to dead center: damage from collision would be too destructive for future life to survive

45. oxygen to nitrogen ratio in atmosphere

    - if larger: advanced life functions would proceed too quickly

    - if smaller: advanced life functions would proceed too slowly

46. carbon dioxide level in atmosphere

    - if greater: runaway greenhouse effect would develop

    - if less: plants would be unable to maintain efficient photosynthesis

47. water vapor level in atmosphere

    - if greater: runaway greenhouse effect would develop

    - if less: rainfall would be too meager for advanced life on the land

48. atmospheric electric discharge rate

- if greater: too much fire destruction would occur

- if less: too little nitrogen would be fixed in the atmosphere

49. ozone level in atmosphere

- if greater: surface temperatures would be too low

- if less: surface temperatures would be too high; there would be too much uv radiation at the surface

50. oxygen quantity in atmosphere

- if greater: plants and hydrocarbons would burn up too easily

- if less: advanced animals would have too little to breathe

51. nitrogen quantity in atmosphere

- if greater: too much buffering of oxygen for advanced animal respiration; too much nitrogen fixation for support of diverse plant species

- if less: too little buffering of oxygen for advanced animal respiration; too little nitrogen fixation for support of diverse plant species

52. ratio of 40K, 235,238U, 232Th to iron for the planet

- if too low: inadequate levels of plate tectonic and volcanic activity

- if too high: radiation, earthquakes, and volcanoes at levels too high for advanced life

53. rate of interior heat loss

- if too low: inadequate energy to drive the required levels of plate tectonic and volcanic activity

- if too high: plate tectonic and volcanic activity shuts down too quickly

54. seismic activity

- if greater: too many life-forms would be destroyed

- if less: nutrients on ocean floors from river runoff would not be recycled to continents through tectonics; not enough carbon dioxide would be released from carbonates

55. volcanic activity

- if lower: insufficient amounts of carbon dioxide and water vapor would be returned to the atmosphere; soil mineralization would become too degraded for life

- if higher: advanced life, at least, would be destroyed

56. rate of decline in tectonic activity

- if slower: advanced life can never survive on the planet

- if faster: advanced life can never survive on the planet

57. rate of decline in volcanic activity

- if slower: advanced life can never survive on the planet

- if faster: advanced life can never survive on the planet

58. timing of birth of continent formation

- if too early: silicate-carbonate cycle would be destabilized

- if too late: silicate-carbonate cycle would be destabilized

59. oceans-to-continents ratio

- if greater: diversity and complexity of life-forms would be limited

- if smaller: diversity and complexity of life-forms would be limited

60. rate of change in oceans-to-continents ratio

- if smaller: advanced life will lack the needed land mass area

- if greater: advanced life would be destroyed by the radical changes

61. global distribution of continents (for Earth)

- if too much in the southern hemisphere: seasonal differences would be too severe for advanced life

62. frequency and extent of ice ages

- if smaller: insufficient fertile, wide, and well-watered valleys produced for diverse and advanced life forms; insufficient mineral concentrations occur for diverse and advanced life

- if greater: planet inevitably experiences runaway freezing

63. soil mineralization

- if too nutrient poor: diversity and complexity of life-forms would be limited

- if too nutrient rich: diversity and complexity of life-forms would be limited

64. gravitational interaction with a moon

- if greater: tidal effects on the oceans, atmosphere, and rotational period would be too severe

- if less: orbital obliquity changes would cause climatic instabilities; movement of nutrients and life from the oceans to the continents and vice versa would be insufficent; magnetic field would be too weak

65. Jupiter distance

- if greater: too many asteroid and comet collisions would occur on Earth

- if less: Earth's orbit would become unstable

66. Jupiter mass

- if greater: Earth's orbit would become unstable

- if less: too many asteroid and comet collisions would occur on Earth

67. drift in major planet distances

- if greater: Earth's orbit would become unstable

- if less: too many asteroid and comet collisions would occur on Earth

68. major planet eccentricities

- if greater: orbit of life supportable planet would be pulled out of life support zone

69. major planet orbital instabilities

- if greater: orbit of life supportable planet would be pulled out of life support zone

70. mass of Neptune

- if too small: not enough Kuiper Belt Objects (asteroids beyond Neptune) would be scattered out of the solar system

- if too large: chaotic resonances among the gas giant planets would occur

71. Kuiper Belt of asteroids (beyond Neptune)

- if not massive enough: Neptune's orbit remains too eccentric which destabilizes the orbits of other solar system planets

- if too massive: too many chaotic resonances and collisions would occur in the solar system

72. separation distances among inner terrestrial planets

- if too small: orbits of all inner planets will become unstable in less than 100,000,000 million years

- if too large: orbits of the most distant from star inner planets will become chaotic

73. atmospheric pressure

- if too small: liquid water will evaporate too easily and condense too infrequently; weather and climate variation would be too extreme; lungs will not function

- if too large: liquid water will not evaporate easily enough for land life; insufficient sunlight reaches planetary surface; insufficient uv radiation reaches planetary surface; insufficient climate and weather variation; lungs will not function

74. atmospheric transparency

- if smaller: insufficient range of wavelengths of solar radiation reaches planetary surface

- if greater: too broad a range of wavelengths of solar radiation reaches planetary surface

75. magnitude and duration of sunspot cycle

- if smaller or shorter: insufficient variation in climate and weather

- if greater or longer: variation in climate and weather would be too much

76. continental relief

- if smaller: insufficient variation in climate and weather

- if greater: variation in climate and weather would be too much

77. chlorine quantity in atmosphere

- if smaller: erosion rates, acidity of rivers, lakes, and soils, and certain metabolic rates would be insufficient for most life forms

- if greater: erosion rates, acidity of rivers, lakes, and soils, and certain metabolic rates would be too high for most life forms

78. iron quantity in oceans and soils

- if smaller: quantity and diversity of life would be too limited for support of advanced life; if very small, no life would be possible

- if larger: iron poisoning of at least advanced life would result

79. tropospheric ozone quantity

- if smaller: insufficient cleansing of biochemical smogs would result

- if larger: respiratory failure of advanced animals, reduced crop yields, and destruction of ozone-sensitive species would result

80. stratospheric ozone quantity

- if smaller: too much uv radiation reaches planet's surface causing skin cancers and reduced plant growth

- if larger: too little uv radiation reaches planet's surface causing reduced plant growth and insufficient vitamin production for animals

81. mesospheric ozone quantity

- if smaller: circulation and chemistry of mesospheric gases so disturbed as to upset relative abundances of life essential gases in lowe atmosphere

- if greater: circulation and chemistry of mesospheric gases so disturbed as to upset relative abundances of life essential gases in lower atmosphere

82. quantity and extent of forest and grass fires

- if smaller: growth inhibitors in the soils would accumulate; soil nitrification would be insufficient; insufficient charcoal production for adequate soil water retention and absorption of certain growth inhibitors

- if greater: too many plant and animal life forms would be destroyed

83. quantity of soil sulfer

- if smaller: plants will become defieient in certain proteins and die

- if larger: plants will die from sulfur toxins; acidity of water and soil will become too great for life; nitrogen cycles will be disturbed

84. biomass to comet infall ratio

- if smaller: greenhouse gases accumulate, triggering runaway surface temperature increase

- if larger: greenhouse gases decline, triggering a runaway freezing

85. density of quasars

  - if smaller: insufficient production and ejection of cosmic dust into the intergalactic medium; ongoing star formation impeded; deadly radiation unblocked

  - if larger: too much cosmic dust forms; too many stars form too late disrupting the formation of a solar-type star at the right time and under the right conditions for life

86. density of giant galaxies in the early universe

  - if smaller: insufficient metals ejected into the intergalactic medium depriving future generations of stars of the metal abundances necessary for a life-support planet at the right time in cosmic history

- if larger: too large a quantity of metals ejected into the intergalactic medium providing future stars with too high of a metallicity for a life-support planet at the right time in cosmic history

87. giant star density in galaxy

- if smaller: insufficient production of galactic dust; ongoing star formation impeded; deadly radiation unblocked

- if larger: too much galactic dust forms; too many stars form too early disrupting the formation of a solar-type star at the right time and under the right conditions for life

88. rate of sedimentary loading at crustal subduction zones

- if smaller: too few instabilities to trigger the movement of crustal plates into the mantle thereby disrupting carbonate-silicate cycle

- if larger: too many instabilities triggering too many crustal plates to move down into the mantle thereby disrupting carbonate-silicate cycle

89. poleward heat transport in planet's atmosphere

- if smaller: disruption of climates and ecosystems; lowered biomass and species diversity; decreased storm activity and precipitation

- if larger: disruption of climates and ecosystems; lowered biomass and species diversity; increased storm activity

90. polycyclic aromatic hydrocarbon abundance in solar nebula

- if smaller: insufficient early production of asteroids which would prevent a planet like Earth from receiving adequate delivery of heavy elements and carbonaceous material for life, advanced life in particular

- if larger: early production of asteroids would be too great resulting in too many collision events striking a planet arising out of the nebula that could support life

91. phosphorus and iron absorption by banded iron formations

    - if smaller: overproduction of cyanobacteria would have consumed too much carbon dioxide and released too much oxygen into Earth's atmosphere thereby overcompensating for the increase in the Sun's luminosity (too much reduction in atmospheric greenhouse efficiency)

    - if larger: underproduction of cyanobacteria would have consumed too little carbon dioxide and released too little oxygen into Earth's atmosphere thereby undercomsating for the increase in the Sun's luminosity (too little reduction in atmospheric greenhouse efficiency)

92. silicate dust annealing by nebular shocks

- if too little: rocky planets with efficient plate tectonics cannot form

- if too much: too many collisions in planetary system.; too severe orbital instabilities in planetary system

93. size of galactic central bulge

- if smaller: inadequate infusion of gas and dust into the spiral arms preventing solar type stars from forming at the right locations late enough in the galaxy's history

- if larger: radiation from the bulge region would kill life on the life-support planet

94. total mass of Kuiper Belt asteroids

- if smaller: Neptune's orbit would not be adequately circularized

- if larger: too severe gravitational instabilities generated in outer solar system

95. solar magnetic activity level

- if greater: solar luminosity fluctuations will be too large

96. number of hypernovae

- if smaller: too little nitrogen is produced in the early universe, thus, cannot get the kinds of stars and planets later in the universe that are necessary for life

- if larger: too much nitrogen is produced in the early universe, thus, cannot get the kinds of stars and planets later in the universe that are necessary for life

97. timing of hypernovae production

- if too early: galaxies become too metal rich too quickly to make stars and planets suitable for life support at the right time

- if too late: insufficient metals available to make quickly enough stars and planets suitable for life support

98. masses of stars that become hypernovae

- if not massive enough: insufficient metals are ejected into the interstellar medium; that is, not enough metals are available for future star generations to make stars and planets suitable for the support of life

- if too massive: all the metals produced by the hypernova eruptions collapse into the black holes resulting from the eruptions; that is, none of the metals are available for future generations of stars

99. quantity of geobacteraceae

- if smaller or non-existent: polycyclic aromatic hydrocarbons accumulate in the surface environment thereby contaminating the environment for other life forms

100. density of brown dwarfs

- if too low: too many low mass stars are produced which will disrupt planetary orbits

- if too high: disruption of planetary orbits

101. quantity of aerobic photoheterotrophic bacteria

- if smaller: inadequate recycling of both organic and inorganic carbon in the oceans

102. average rainfall preciptiation

- if too small: inadequate water supplies for land-based life; inadequate erosion of land masses to sustain the carbonate-silicate cycle.; inadequate erosion to sustain certain species of ocean life that are vital for the existence of all life

- if too large: too much erosion of land masses which upsets the carbonate-silicate cycle and hastens the extinction of many species of life that are vital for the existence of all life

103. variation and timing of average rainfall precipitation

- if too small or at the wrong time: erosion rates that upset the carbonate-silicate cycle and fail to adjust adequately the planet's atmosphere for the increase in the sun's luminosity

- if too large or at the wrong time: erosion rates that upset the carbonate-silicate cycle and fail to adjust the planet's atmosphere for the increase in the sun's luminosity

104. average slope or relief of the continental land masses

- if too small: inadequate erosion

- if too large: too much erosion

105. distance from nearest black hole

- if too close: radiation will prove deadly for life

106. absorption rate of planets and planetismals by parent star

   - if too low: disturbs sun's luminosity and stability of sun's long term luminosity

   - if too high: disturbs orbits of inner solar system planets; disturbs sun's luminosity and stability of sun's long term luminosity

107. water absorption capacity of planet's lower mantle

   - if too low: too much water on planet's surface; no continental land masses; too little plate tectonic activity; carbonate-silicate cycle disrupted

   - if too high: too little water on planet's surface; too little plate tectonic activity; carbonate-silicate cycle disrupted

108. gas dispersal rate by companion stars, shock waves, and molecular cloud expansion in the Sun's birthing star cluster

- if too low: too many stars form in Sun's vicinity which will disturb planetary orbits and pose a radiation problem; too much gas and dust in solar system's vicinity

- if too high: not enough gas and dust condensation for the Sun and its planets to form; insufficient gas and dust in solar system's vicinity

109. decay rate of cold dark matter particles

- if too low: insufficient production of dwarf spheroidal galaxies which will limit the maintenance of long-lived large spiral galaxies

- if too high: too many dwarf spheroidal galaxies produced which will cause spiral galaxies to be too unstable

110. ratio of inner dark halo mass to stellar mass for galaxy

- if too low: corotation distance is too close to the center of the galaxy which exposes the life-support planet to too much radiation and too many gravitational disturbances

- if too high: corotation distance is too far from the center of the galaxy where the abundance of heavy elements is too sparse to make rocky planets

111. star rotation rate

- if too slow: too weak of a magnetic field resulting in not enough protection from cosmic rays for the life-support planet

- if too fast: too much chromospheric emission causing radiation problems for the life-support planet

112. rate of nearby gamma ray bursts

- if too low: insufficient mass extinctions of life to create new habitats for more advanced species

- if too high: too many mass extinctions of life for the maintenance of long-lived species

113. aerosol particle density emitted from forests

- if too low: too little cloud condensation which reduces rainfall, lowers the albedo (planetary reflectivity), and disturbs climates on a global scale

- if too high: too much cloud condensation which increases rainfall, raises the albedo (planetary reflectivity), and disturbs climate on a global scale; too much smog

114. density of interstellar and interplanetary dust particles in vicinity of life-support planet

- if too low: inadequate delivery of life-essential materials

- if too high: disturbs climate too radically on life-support planet

115. thickness of mid-mantle boundary

- if too thin: mantle convection eddies become too strong; tectonic activity and silicate production become too great

- if too thick: mantle convection eddies become too weak; tectonic activity and silicate production become too small

116. galaxy cluster density

- if too low: insufficient infall of gas, dust, and dwarf galaxies into a large galaxy that eventually could form a life-supportable planet

- if too high: gravitational influences from nearby galaxies will disturb orbit of the star that has a life-supprtable planet thereby exposing that planet either to deadly radiation or to gravitational disturbances from other stars in that galaxy

117. star formation rate in solar neighborhood during past 4 billion years

- if too high: life on Earth will be exposed to deadly radiation or orbit of Earth will be disturbed

118. variation in star formation rate in solar neighborhood during past 4 billion years

- if too high: life on Earth will be exposed to deadly radiation or orbit of Earth will be disturbed

119. gamma-ray burst events

- if too few: not enough production of copper, scandium, titanium, and zinc

- if too many: too many mass extinction events

120. cosmic ray luminosity of Milky Way Galaxy:

- if too low: not enough production of boron

- if too high: life spans for advanced life too short; too much destruction of planet's ozone layer

121. air turbulence in troposphere

   - if too low: inadequate formation of water droplets

   - if too great: rainfall distribution will be too uneven

122. primordial cosmic superwinds

   - if too low of an intensity: inadequate star formation late in cosmic history

   - if too great of an intensity: inadequate star formation early in cosmic history

123. smoking quasars

   - if too few: inadequate primordial dust production for stimulating future star formation

   - if too many: early star formation will be too vigorous resulting in too few stars and planets being able to form late in cosmic history

124. quantity of phytoplankton

- if too low; inadequate production of molecular oxygen and inadequate production of maritime sulfate aerosols (cloud condensation nuclei); inadequate consumption of carbon dioxide

- if too great: too much cooling of sea surface waters and possibly too much reduction of ozone quantity in lower stratosphere; too much consumption of carbon dioxide

125. quantity of iodocarbon-emitting marine organisms

- if too low: inadequate marine cloud cover; inadequate water cycling

- if too great: too much marine cloud cover; too much cooling of Earth's surface

126. mantle plume production

- if too low: inadequate volcanic and island production rate

- if too great: too much destruction and atmospheric disturbance from volcanic eruptions

127. quantity of magnetars (proto-neutron stars with very strong magnetic fields)

- if too few during galaxy's history: inadequate quantities of r-process elements are synthesized

- if too many during galaxy's history: too great a quantity of r-process elements are synthesized; too great of a high-energy cosmic ray production

128. frequency of gamma ray bursts in galaxy

- if too low: inadequate production of copper, titanium, and zinc; insufficient hemisphere-wide mass extinction events

- if too great: too much production of copper and zinc; too many hemisphere-wide mass extinction events

129.   parent star magnetic field

- if too low: solar wind and solar magnetosphere will not be adequate to thwart a significant amount of cosmic rays

- if too great: too high of an x-ray flux will be generated

130.   amount of outward migration of Neptune

- if too low: total mass of Kuiper Belt objects will be too great; Kuiper Belt will be too close to the sun; Neptune's orbit will not be circular enough and distant enough to guarantee long-term stability of inner solar system planets' orbits

- if too great: Kuiper Belt will be too distant and contain too little mass to play any significant role in contributing volatiles to life-support planet or to contributing to mass extinction events; Neptune will be too distant to play a role in contributing to the long-term stability of inner solar system planets' orbits

131. Q-value (rigidity) of Earth during its early history

- if too low: final obliquity of Earth becomes too high; rotational braking of Earth too low

- if too great: final obliquity of Earth becomes too low; rotational braking of Earth is too great

132. parent star distance from galaxy's corotation circle

- if too close: a strong mean motion resonance will destabilize the parent star's galactic orbit

- if too far: planetary system will experience too many crossings of the spiral arms

133. average quantity of gas infused into the universe's first star clusters

- if too small: wind form supergiant stars in the clusters will blow the clusters apart which in turn will prevent or seriously delay the formation of galaxies

- if too large: early star formation, black hole production, and galaxy formation will be too vigorous for spiral galaxies to persist long enough for the right kinds of stars and planets to form so that life will be possible

134. frequency of late impacts by large asteroids and comets

- if too low: too few mass extinction events; inadequate rich ore deposits of ferrous and heavy metals

- if too many: too many mass extinction events; too radical of disturbances of planet's crust

135. level of supersonic turbulence in the infant universe

- if too low: first stars will be of the wrong type and quantity to produce the necessary mix of elements, gas, and dust so that a future star and planetary system capable of supporting life will appear at the right time in cosmic history

- if too high: first stars will be of the wrong type and quantity to produce the necessary mix of elements, gas, and dust so that a future star and planetary system capable of supporting life will appear at the right time in cosmic history

136. number density of the first metal-free stars to form in the universe

- if too low: inadequate initial production of heavy elements and dust by these stars to foster the necessary future star formations that will lead to a possible life-support body

- if too many: super winds blown out by these stars will prevent or seriously delay the formation of the kinds of galaxies that could possibly produce a future life-support body

137. size of the carbon sink in the deep mantle of the planet

  - if too small: carbon dioxide level in planet's atmosphere will be too high

  - if too large: carbon dioxide level in planet's atmosphere will be too low; biomass will be too small

138. rate of growth of central spheroid for the galaxy

  - if too small: inadequate flow of heavy elements into the spiral disk; inadequate outward drift of stars from the inner to the central portions of the spiral disk

  - if too large: inadequate spiral disk of late-born stars

139. amount of gas infalling into the central core of the galaxy

- if too little: galaxy's nuclear bulge becomes too large

- if too much: galaxy's nuclear bulge fails to become large enough

140. level of cooling of gas infalling into the central core of the galaxy

- if too low: galaxy's nuclear bulge becomes too large

- if too high: galaxy's nuclear bulge fails to become large enough

141. ratio of dual water molecules, $(H_2O)_2$, to single water molecules, H_2O, in the troposphere

- if too low: inadequate raindrop formation; inadequate rainfall

- if too high: too uneven of a distribution of rainfall over planet's surface

142. heavy element abundance in the intracluster medium for the early universe

- if too low: too much star formation too early in cosmic history; no life-support body will ever form or it will form at the wrong tine and/or place

- if too high: inadequate star formation early in cosmic history; no life-support body will ever form or it will form at the wrong tine and/or place

143. quantity of volatiles on and in Earth-sized planet in the habitable zone

- if too low: inadequate ingredients for the support of life

- if too high: no possibility for a means to compensate for luminosity changes in star

144. pressure of the intra-galaxy-cluster medium

- if too low: inadequate star formation bursts in large galaxies

- if too high: star formation burst activity in large galaxies is too aggressive, too frequent, and too early in cosmic history

145. level of spiral substructure in spiral galaxy

    - if too low: galaxy will not be old enough to sustain advanced life

    - if too high: gravitational chaos will disturb planetary system's orbit about center of galaxy and thereby expose the planetary system to deadly radiation and/or disturbances by gas or dust clouds

146. mass of outer gas giant planet relative to inner gas giant planet

    - if greater than 50 percent: resonances will generate non-coplanar planetary orbits which will destabilize orbit of life-support planet

    - if less than 25 percent: mass of the inner gas giant planet necessary to adequately protect life-support planet from asteroidal and cometary collisions would be large enough to gravitationally disturb the orbit of the life-support planet

147. triggering of El Nino events by explosive volcanic eruptions

- if too seldom: uneven rainfall distribution over continental land masses

- if too frequent: uneven rainfall distribution over continental land masses; too much destruction by the volcanic events; drop in mean global surface temperature

148. time window between the peak of kerogen production and the appearance of intelligent life

- if too short: inadequate time for geological and chemical processes to transform the kerogen into enough petroleum reserves to launch and sustain advanced civilization

- if too long: too much of the petroleum reserves will be broken down by bacterial activity into methane

149. time window between the production of cisterns in the planet's crust that can effectively collect and store petroleum and natural gas and the appearance of intelligent life

    - if too short: inadequate time for collecting and storing significant amounts of petroleum and natural gas

    - if too long: too many leaks form in the cisterns which lead to the dissipation of petroleum and gas

150. efficiency of flows of silicate melt, hypersaline hydrothermal fluids, and hydrothermal vapors in the upper crust

    - if too low: inadequate crystallization and precipitation of concentrated metal ores that can be exploited by intelligent life to launch civilization and technology

- if too high: crustal environment becomes too unstable for the maintenance of civilization

151. quantity of dust formed in the ejecta of Population III supernovae

- if too low: number and mass range of Population II stars will not be great enough for a life-support planet to form at the right time and place in the cosmos; Population II stars will not form soon enough after the appearance of Population III stars

- if too high: Population II star formation will occur too soon and be too aggressive for a life-support planet to form at the right time and place in the cosmos

152. quantity and proximity of gamma-ray burst events relative to emerging solar nebula

- if too few and too far: inadequate enrichment of solar nebula with copper, titanium, and zinc

- if too many and too close: too much enrichment of solar nebula with copper and zinc; too much destruction of solar nebula

153. heat flow through the planet's mantle from radiometric decay in planet's core

  - if too low: mantle will be too viscous and, thus, mantle convection will not be vigorous enough to drive plate tectonics at the precise level to compensate for changes in star's luminosity

  - if too high: mantle will not be viscous enough and, thus, mantle convection will be too vigorous resulting in too high of a level of plate tectonic activity to perfectly compensate for changes in star's luminosity

154. water absorption by planet's mantle

  - if too low: mantle will be too viscous and, thus, mantle convection will not be vigorous enough to drive plate tectonics at the precise level to compensate for changes in star's luminosity

- if too high: mantle will not be viscous enough and, thus, mantle convection will be too vigorous resulting in too high of a level of plate tectonic activity to perfectly compensate for changes in star's luminosity

Keep in mind that this list is always growing as new improbabilities are being discovered. According to Dr.'s Ross and Rana, the improbability increases by about a million times each month! There are really three possibilities that could have resulted in this incredible fine-tuning; *law*, *chance* or *design*. Scientists have puzzled over it for years and have found no natural laws that can account for it. The odds against such a theory ever being discovered seem insurmountable. Even Stephen Hawking, who was originally a believer in a "Theory of Everything" that could possibly explain the fine-tuning as necessary by law, after considering Gödel's

Theorem concluded that one was not obtainable. He states:

> *Some people will be very disappointed if there is not an ultimate theory which can be formulated as a finite number of principles. I used to belong to that camp, but I have changed my mind.* (3)

Since the threshold of mathematical impossibility is 1 in 10 to the 50th power (ie: given a 13.73 billion year universe, there is not enough time for anything with this or smaller odds to occur by chance), and the odds of this fine-tuning coming into existence by chance are far, far beyond that, we can rule out chance. Only a transcendent Creator makes sense of this unbelievably complex order in the universe.

During the last 35 years or so, scientists have discovered that the existence of intelligent life absolutely depends upon this very delicate and complex balance of initial conditions. It appears that "the deck was stacked" in the substances, constants and quantities of the Big Bang itself, to provide a life-permitting universe. We now know through modern science that life-prohibiting universes are vastly more probable than any life-permitting universe like ours. How much more probable?

Well, the answer is that the chances that the universe should be life-permitting are so infinitesimally small as to be incomprehensible and incalculable. For example, Stephen Hawking has estimated that if the rate of the universe's expansion one second after the Big Bang had been smaller by even one part in a hundred thousand million million, the universe would have re-collapsed into a hot fireball due to gravitational attraction. (4) Physicist P.C.W. Davies has calculated that the odds against the initial conditions being suitable for star formation (without which planets could not exist) is one followed by at least a thousand billion billion zeroes! (5) Davies also calculates that a change in the strength of gravity or of the weak force by merely one part in 10 raised to the 100th power (!) would have prevented a life-permitting universe. (6) As we saw in the previous lists, there are dozens and dozens of such constants and quantities present in the Big Bang which must be exquisitely fine-tuned in this way if the universe is to permit life. Moreover, it's not only each individual quantity or constant which must be finely tuned; their ratios to each other must also be exquisitely finely tuned. Therefore, vast improbability is multiplied by vast improbability, and yet again by vast improbability repeatedly until our minds are simply reeling in vanishingly small odds.

There is no plausible physical reason why these constants and quantities should have the values that they do. Reflecting on this, the once-agnostic physicist P.C.W. Davies comments, "Through my scientific work I have come to believe more and more strongly that the physical universe is put together with an ingenuity so astonishing that I cannot accept it merely as a brute fact." (7) Likewise, British Astrophysicist Sir Frederick Hoyle remarks, "A common sense interpretation of the facts suggests that a super-intellect has monkeyed with physics." (8) Robert Jastrow, the head of NASA's Goddard Institute for Space Studies, refers to this as "the most powerful evidence for the existence of God ever to come out of science." (9)

So, again, the view that Christian theists have historically held, that there is an intelligent Designer of the universe, seems to make so much more sense than the atheistic alternative: that the universe, when it popped into being, without cause, out of nothing, just happened to be, by chance, fine-tuned for intelligent life with a mind-numbingly unlikely precision and delicacy. To call the odds against this fine-tuning occurring by chance "astronomical" would be a wild understatement. One might reduce it to a propositional argument as follows:

Teleological Argument

1. The fine-tuning of the universe is due to either law, chance, or design.

2. It is not due to law or chance.

3. Therefore, it is due to design.

Entropy

As we discussed in Chapter One, the term "entropy" describes the degree of thermodynamic "disorder" in a closed system like the universe. "Maximum entropy" would describe the "heat death" of the universe (which is the state it is slowly gravitating towards). Amazingly, our universe was at its "minimum entropy" at the very beginning, which begs the question "how did it get so orderly?" Looking just at the initial entropy conditions, what is the likelihood of a universe supportive of life coming into existence by coincidence? One in billions of billions? Or trillions of trillions of trillions? Or more?

Roger Penrose, a famous British mathematician and a close friend of Stephen Hawking, wondered about this question and tried to calculate the probability of the initial entropy conditions of the Big Bang.

According to Penrose, the odds against such an occurrence were on the order of 1 in 10 to the power of 10 to the power of 123 (1 in 10^{10} to the 123rd power).

It is so large that it's hard even to imagine what this number means. We can use "superscript" to indicate the order of magnitude (the little raised 10 in the above paragraph), but we'd need "super-superscript" to properly write the "123" following it (the program I'm using to write this can't do that, so I write it out the long way). In math, the value 10 to the 123rd power means 1 followed by 123 zeros. (This is, by the way, more than the total number of atoms [10 to the 79th power] believed to exist in the whole universe.) But Penrose's answer is vastly more than this: It requires 1 followed by 10^{123} zeros!

Or consider it this way: 10 to the 3rd power means "1,000". 10 to the 10 to the 3rd power is a number that has 1 followed by 1000 zeros. If there are six zeros, it's called a million; if nine, a billion; if twelve, a trillion and so on. There is not even a name for a number that has 1 followed by 10 to the 123rd power zeros.

In practical terms, in probability theory, odds of less than 1 in 10 to the 50th power = "zero probability". Penrose's number is more than a trillion, trillion, trillion times less than that. In short, Penrose's number tells us that the "accidental" or "coincidental" creation of our universe is an impossibility.

Concerning this mind-boggling number Roger Penrose comments:

> *This now tells how precise the Creator's aim must have been, namely to an accuracy of one part in*

10 to the 10^{123}. This is an extraordinary figure. One could not possibly even write the number down in full in the ordinary denary notation: it would be 1 followed by 10^{123} successive 0's. (10)

Even if we were to write a 0 on each separate proton and on each separate neutron in the entire universe - and we could throw in all the other particles for good measure - we would fall far short of writing down the figure needed.

It takes far more "faith" to believe that this happened by chance than to believe that it was instigated by an incredibly powerful mind. The latter inference does not require blind faith!

It's important to recognize that we're not talking about a single unlikely event here. We're talking about hitting the jackpot over and over again, nailing extremely unlikely, mutually complementary parameters of constants and quantities, far past the point where chance could account for it.

The secular science community has coined a term for this incredible fine-tuning: the "Anthropic Principle". Their position, which is clearly steered by atheistic philosophy instead of an honest inference to the best explanation, is that life has evolved within all of these incredibly tight parameters by chance, and that we should not be surprised that the parameters are precise, as otherwise we would not exist to observe them. Christian philosopher William Lane Craig has pointed out that this is an error in reasoning. While it's true that inasmuch as we are alive, we should not be surprised that we do observe things, we should be surprised that we are alive at all to observe anything. This can be clearly seen by means of an illustration (borrowed from John Leslie): suppose you are dragged before a firing squad of 100 trained marksmen, all of them with rifles aimed at your heart, to be executed. The command is given; you hear the deafening sound of the guns. And you observe that you are still alive, that all of the 100 marksmen missed! Now while it is true that:

1. You should not be surprised that you do not

observe that you are dead,
nonetheless it is equally true that:

2. Given the fact that 100 marksmen were aiming for you, you should be surprised that you do observe that you are alive.

Since the firing squad's missing you altogether is extremely improbable, the surprise expressed is wholly appropriate, though you are not surprised that you do not observe that you are dead, since if you were dead you could not observe it. Similarly, while we should not be surprised that we do not observe features of the universe which are incompatible with our existence, it is nevertheless true that we should be surprised that we do observe features of the universe which are compatible with our existence, in view of the enormous improbabilities thereof.

In other words, in view of the enormous improbability that the universe would be compatible with our existence, we should be surprised that we observe a universe that is finely-tuned to allow for it.

It is instructive to note that one of the developers of the "Anthropic Principle" concept, Dr. Frank Tipler, has become a Christian since that time, due in large part to reflections on the overwhelming evidence for a Designer from nature.

One question that is often raised subsequent to hearing of the fine-tuning of the universe is "if the parameters were different, why couldn't life have evolved within the different parameters?" The answer to that is that life cannot evolve even under the most ideal of conditions—the irreducible and specified complexity of life has disproven Darwinian evolution (we'll discuss that in more detail later). Although micro-evolution (small changes within a species or "kind") has been observed and does occur in nature, it always results in a loss or lateral drift in information. It never results in an increase in information. The media and many philosophically driven scientists ascribe tremendous flexibility to the idea of micro-evolution, many claiming or assuming that macro-evolution is simply a result of large quantities of micro-evolution, but this has been shown to be impossible under every kind of testing. Darwinian, or macro-evolution, has not been reproducible under even the most artificially ideal conditions in the laboratory. Moreover, changes in most of the aforementioned parameters of fine-tuning would result in no planetary habitat forming that could support life, which eliminates the possibility of life before we even get to the insurmountable problem of biological assembly.

Take a look at the assessments of some noted scientists regarding this fine-tuning, beginning with a pair of Albert Einstein quotes (as harmonized by Matt Barber):

Albert Einstein, who is often falsely characterized as having been an atheist, once said of non-believers: "The fanatical atheists are like slaves who are still feeling the weight of their chains which they have thrown off after hard struggle. They are creatures who – in their grudge against traditional religion as the 'opium of the masses' — cannot hear the music of the spheres."

Indeed, Psalm 19:1 observes: "The heavens declare the glory of God; the skies proclaim the work of his hands."

Einstein addressed the inherent hubris associated with God-denial:

I'm not an atheist. I don't think I can call myself a pantheist. The problem involved is too vast for our limited minds. We are in the position of a little child entering a huge library filled with books in many languages. The child knows someone must have written those books. It does not know how. It does not understand the languages in which they are written. The child dimly suspects a mysterious order in the arrangement of the books but doesn't know what it is. That, it seems to me, is the attitude of even the most intelligent human being toward God. We see the universe marvelously arranged and obeying certain laws but only dimly understand these laws. (11)

Sir Frederick Hoyle (British Astrophysicist): "A common sense interpretation of the facts suggests that a superintellect has monkeyed with physics, as well as with chemistry and biology, and that there are no blind forces worth speaking about in nature. The numbers one calculates from the facts seem to me so overwhelming as to put this conclusion almost beyond question." (12)

Dr. George Ellis (South African Astrophysicist, and collaborator on the Hawking-Penrose Singularity Theorems): "Amazing fine tuning occurs in the laws that make this [complexity] possible. Realization of the complexity of what is accomplished makes it very difficult not to use the word 'miraculous' without taking a stand as to the ontological status of the word." (13)

And on several other occasions: "God is the creator and sustainer of the universe and of humankind, transcending the universe but immanent in it."

"God's nature embodies justice and holiness, but is also a personal and loving God who cares for each creature (so the name "father" is indeed appropriate)."

"God's nature is revealed most perfectly in the life and teachings of Jesus of Nazareth, as recorded in the New Testament of the Bible, who was sent by God to reveal the divine nature, summarized in "God is Love."

"God has an active presence in the world that still touches the lives of the faithful today." (14)

Dr. Paul Davies (British Astrophysicist, and Professor at Arizona State University): "There is for me powerful evidence that there is something going on behind it all....It seems as though somebody has fine-tuned nature's numbers to make the Universe....The impression of design is overwhelming". (15) And:

"The laws [of physics] ... seem to be the product of exceedingly ingenious design... The universe must have a purpose". (16)

Dr. Alan Sandage (Astronomer at Carnegie Observatories, winner of the Crawford prize in astronomy): "I find it quite improbable that such order came out of chaos. There has to be some organizing principle. God to me is a mystery but is the explanation for the miracle of existence, why there is something instead of nothing." (17)

Dr. John O'Keefe (Astronomer at NASA): "We are, by astronomical standards, a pampered, cosseted, cherished group of creatures.. .. If the Universe had not been made with the most exacting precision we could never have come into existence. It is my view that these circumstances indicate the universe was created for man to live in." (18)

Dr. Tony Rothman (Physicist, former editor of Scientific American): "When confronted with the order and beauty of the universe and the strange coincidences of nature, it's very tempting to take the leap of faith from science into religion.

I am sure many physicists want to. I only wish they would admit it." (19)

Dr. Vera Kistiakowsky (MIT professor of Physics): "The exquisite order displayed by our scientific understanding of the physical world calls for the divine." (20)

Dr. Ed Harrison (former NASA cosmologist, Professor at U. Mass.): "Here is the cosmological proof of the existence of God – the design argument of Paley – updated and refurbished. The fine tuning of the universe provides prima facie evidence of deistic design. Take your choice: blind chance that requires multitudes of universes or design that requires only one.... Many scientists, when they admit their views, incline toward the teleological or design argument." (21)

Dr. Barry Parker (American Particle Physicist): "Who created these laws? There is no question but that a God will always be needed." (22)

Drs. Idit Zehavi, and Avishai Dekel (Israeli Professors of Astronomy and Physics): "This type of universe, however, seems to require a degree of fine tuning of the initial conditions that is in apparent conflict with 'common wisdom'." (23)

Dr. Henry "Fritz" Schaefer (5 time Nobel Prize nominee, Graham Perdue Professor of Chemistry, and director of the Center for Computational Quantum Chemistry at the University of Georgia): "The significance and joy in my science comes in those occasional moments of discovering something new and saying to myself, 'So that's how God did it.' My goal is to understand a little corner of God's plan." (24)

Dr. Carl Woese (Microbiologist and Physicist, University of Illinois) "Life in Universe - rare or unique? I walk both sides of that street. One day I can say that given the 100 billion stars in our galaxy and the 100 billion or more galaxies, there have to be some planets that formed and evolved in ways very, very like the Earth has, and so would contain microbial life at least. There are other days when I say that the anthropic principal, which makes this universe a special one out of an uncountably large number of universes, may not apply only to that aspect of nature we define in the realm of physics, but may extend to chemistry and biology. In that case life on Earth could be entirely unique." (25)

Dr. Arno Penzias (Nobel prize winner in physics, co-discoverer of the background microwave radiation in the universe proving the Big Bang model): "The best data we have [concerning the Big Bang] are exactly what I would have predicted, had I nothing to go on but the five books of Moses, the Psalms, the Bible as a whole". (26)

In a subsequent radio interview, Penzias was asked what there was before the Big Bang. "We don't know, but we can reasonably say that there was nothing." He replied. An upset listener called immediately, accusing Penzias of being an atheist. He wisely replied: "Madame, I believe you are not aware of the consequences of what I just said. Before the Big Bang there was nothing of what now exists. Had there been something, the question could be: where did it come from?" He continued commenting that if there was nothing and suddenly things began to appear, that was sign that Somebody had taken them from nothing, and concluded saying that his discovery could bring about the overcoming of the historic enmity between science and religion. (27)

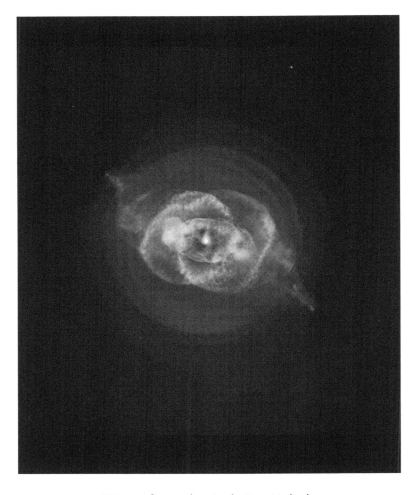

X-Rays from the Cat's Eye Nebula

NASA/CXC/SAO

CHAPTER THREE: THE "HARDWARE" OF LIFE ARGUMENT

"I can see the fingerprints of God
When I look at you
I can see the fingerprints of God
And I know its true
You're a masterpiece
That all creation quietly applauds
And you're covered with the fingerprints of God"

~from *Fingerprints of God*, by Stephen Curtis Chapman

The motherboard from a Sony PlayStation, Wikimedia Commons

The common scientific view of the "hardware of life" (that is, the physical components of living systems) is, as Biologist Richard Dawkins puts it, "the study of complicated things that give the appearance of having been designed for a purpose." (The Blind Watchmaker, 1986).

Unfortunately, Dawkins (like many others in his field) has succumbed to a logically fallacious assumption that a supernatural explanation is not within the "pool of live options" to explain this appearance of design. Why not? Well, to summarize the common opinions of materialists like Dawkins, it's "not science". But what is "Science"?

Louis Pasteur once said "Religions, philosophies, atheism, materialism, or its opposite--none of these is relevant to the matter...I might even add that, scientifically speaking, I am indifferent to them all. The question is purely one of fact". In other words, science should be "the un-biased search for truth" without philosophical preconceptions. That definition was always the ancient understanding of the term.

Since the so-called "Enlightenment" that swept through Europe in the 1700's, and especially since the proposal of Darwin's Theory of Evolution in 1859, however, intellectual activists have been trying to add the qualifying concept of "within naturalistic explanations" to the definition. What that means, in effect, is the addition of a bias to the search for truth.

This bias first "got its legs" from the writings of an apparently bitter atheistic Scottish philosopher named David Hume in the 1700's. Hume proposed a set of reasons why the supernatural should be ruled be ruled out of consideration as an explanatory mechanism. Not long afterwards, these reasons were shown to be fallacious (we'll examine this in a later chapter), but at the time, it was as if Europe was eager to unfetter itself from religion, and atheism blossomed somewhat throughout the continent.

Most modern philosophers (even agnostic ones) find Hume's arguments to be almost laughably illogical, but many atheists unknowingly cite him today as if he was "the Christ" of their belief system. For a full-length treatment of this subject, see John Earman's book *Hume's Abject Failure*, but suffice it to say for the moment that modern humankind has nowhere near a broad enough scope of reality to eliminate the possibility of the supernatural. To the contrary, there are many things in our experience that defy naturalistic explanations.

The philosophical name of the most common scientific form of atheism is "Materialism", and it claims that not only is there no God, but that there is nothing even *like* God in the universe. Although it has taken root within the Biological sciences, it has done so to a much lesser extent within Astronomy, Philosophy, and Physics. Many Americans would probably be surprised to know that polls show that the percentage of PhD'ed scientists overall who identify themselves as Christians and who go to church is roughly the same as the percentage in the population at large. Unfortunately, the small minority who identify themselves as atheists is much louder and more aggressive though, so they exert a disproportionate influence on the media, academic standards committees and the like.

Luckily for all who respect unbiased inquiry, many Philosophers who are experts in logic by definition (logic being a subset of Philosophy), have objected vociferously, especially in the past 40 years, to this effort, and have recognized that the scientific method is at stake. As I wrote before, it seems that the key element that catalyzed this mindset since the late 1800's is Charles Darwin's Theory of Evolution. Biologists became so enamored with it over the years that they invested heavily in deepening and entrenching their paradigms based on that assumption, and are not willing to consider that major problems have developed within it. Pride in Biology, and a reluctance to admit being wrong might be a factor. One has to wonder if there are spiritual and carnal reasons that admitting the mere possibility of the existence of the metaphysical is so daunting to some. Since Darwinian Evolution seems to be the lynchpin of this type of thinking, let's take a hard look at it.

The concept of life arising from non-life by random chance is called "abiogenesis". This concept is the "creation story" of Darwinian Evolution. But what are the odds of the building blocks of life coming together by random chance in a way to provide even the possibility of life? Some years ago, NASA (curious about what might be found in outer space) inquired of Dr. Harold Morowitz, an agnostic Yale University physicist to estimate it. Morowitz created mathematical models by imagining broths of living bacteria that were superheated until all of the complex chemicals were broken down into basic building blocks. After cooling the mixtures, Morowitz used physics calculations to conclude that the odds of a single bacterium reassembling by chance -- under ideal natural conditions -- is one in $10^{100,000,000,000}$! He did another calculation (apparently assuming conditions so idealized that they would not be expected in nature) and came up with a probability of $10^{339,999,866}$. (1) Just to make sure we're being as generous as possible, we'll use the latter probability.

Wow! How can we grasp such a large statistic? Well, it's more likely that one would win the state lottery every week for a million years by purchasing just one ticket each week!

Let's keep in mind that the assumptions Morowitz used were incredibly generous. As Dr. Noam Lavav (an atheist Origin of Life researcher) has stated:

So far, no geochemical evidence for the existence of a prebiotic soup has been published. Indeed, a number of scientists have challenged the prebiotic soup concept, noting that even if it existed, the concentration of organic building blocks in it would have been too small to be meaningful for prebiotic evolution.(*Biogenesis: Theories of Life's Origins,* Oxford University Press, 1999, p138-139)

Yet somehow the materialists still insist that it must have happened that way, because recognizing the impossibility might "allow a Divine foot in the door". This is not sound thinking – this is ideology gone perverse, filtering truth out in order to maintain a preferred worldview.

This is probably a good time to mention that all the evidence indicates that the first cell was about as complex as a modern simple cell. How complex is that? Modern cells contain numerous mind-boggling features. According to

Professor Donald Johnson (who has two earned PhD's; one in Chemistry and one in Computer and Information Sciences), your body has literally hundreds of quadrillions of computers in it, some operating with triple layers of encryption! Also:

- the genetic system IS a pre-existing *operating system*;
- the specific *genetic program* (genome) is an application;
- the *native language* has a *codon-based encryption system*;
- the codes are *read* by *enzyme computers* with their own *operating system*;
- each enzyme's output is to *another operating system* in a ribosome;
- codes are *decrypted* and output to *tRNA computers*;
- each *codon-specified* amino acid is transported to a protein construction site; and
- in each cell, there are *multiple operating systems, multiple programming languages, encoding/decoding hardware and software, specialized communications systems, error detection/correction systems, specialized*

input/output for organelle control and feedback, and a variety of *specialized "devices"* to accomplish the tasks of life. (Dr. Donald E. Johnson – who has earned PhD's in Chemistry and Computer Science -- via Uncommon Descent).

As astonishing as this is, there's more. There are overlapping codes, and codes within codes within codes. Some codes extend epigenetically (beyond the genes), and some rely on combinations of genes being switched on and off. Consider this quote in New Scientist:

A single gene can potentially code for tens of thousands of different proteins... It's the way in which genes are switched on and off, though, that has turned out to be really mind-boggling, with layer after layer of complexity emerging. (~Le Page, "Genome at 10," New Scientist, 6/16/10).

The idea of this stunning array of features developing in a "bottom-up" fashion seems so improbable that words seem inadequate to describe it Given this incredible improbability, one would think that it took an incredibly long time, but that was not available. Earth sustained a prolonged and intense showering of asteroids beginning about 4.1 billion years ago until about 3.8 billion years ago. This event, known as the "Late Heavy Bombardment", rendered life impossible, as the earth's surface was a virtual "sea of magma" (along with other substances hostile to life, like smoke, noxious gasses and radiation) until it let up. Amazingly, however, the first traces of life appear in the fossil record not long after this time! As Paleontologist J. William Schopf has marveled, "no one had foreseen that the beginning of life occurred so astonishingly early." [J. William Schopf, *Cradle of Life (Princeton, NJ: Princeton University Press, 1999), 3.*]

In response to the probabilities calculated by Morowitz, Robert Shapiro, author of *Origins - A Skeptic's Guide to the Creation of Life on Earth*, wrote:

The improbability involved in generating even one bacterium is so large that it reduces all considerations of time and space to nothingness. Given such odds, the time until the black holes evaporate and the space to the ends of the universe would make no difference at all. If we were to wait, we would truly be waiting for a miracle. (2)

Sir Frederick Hoyle compared the probability of life arising by chance to lining up 10^{50} (ten with fifty zeros after it) blind people, giving each one a scrambled Rubik's Cube, and finding that they all solve the cube at the same moment!

Biological "Hardware" (Complex Structure) Argument

1. According to a leading Darwinist, the odds of component parts in close proximity assembling into a single-celled creature are 1 in $10^{339,999,866}$.

2. According to probability theorists, anything with lower odds than 1 in 10^{50} is mathematically impossible.

3. Therefore, the spontaneous generation of life is mathematically impossible.

Regarding the origin of life, Francis Crick, winner of the Nobel Prize in biology for his work with the DNA molecule, stated in 1982:

An honest man, armed with all the knowledge available to us now, could only state that in some sense, the origin of life appears at the moment

to be almost a miracle, so many are
the conditions which would have had
to have been satisfied to get it going.
(3)

Crick's assessment of the hopelessness of the spontaneous generation of life on earth led him to subsequently postulate a theory called "Directed Panspermia", which held that space aliens "seeded" life on earth. As Philip Johnson observed, "When a scientist of Crick's caliber feels he has to invoke undetectable spaceman, it is time to consider whether the field of prebiological evolution has come to a dead end." (4)

Ever since the discovery of DNA in 1953, the Darwinian Theory of Evolution has faced increasing challenges yearly as more and more evidence for the complexity of the cell has been discovered. In 1996, Dr. Michael Behe (professor of Biochemistry at Lehigh University) released a book entitled "Darwins' Black Box", which detailed an argument against Darwinian Evolution known as the "irreducible complexity" of biological structures and systems. In the 11 years since the publication of the book, it has been attacked from every angle by atheistic scientists, yet its central thesis has only gained strength, as the debate has exposed the weakness of Darwinian counter-arguments, and the naturalistic (atheistic) philosophical biases that lurk behind them.

Have you ever wondered if Charles Darwin himself would still believe in Darwinian Evolution (or macro-evolution) if he knew all of the evidence that has accumulated for and against it up to this time? Well, there is an interesting quote in which Darwin stated his own minimum standard for assessing whether or not his theory would withstand the tests of time:

> *If it could be demonstrated that any complex organ existed, which could not possibly have been formed by numerous, successive, slight modifications, my theory would absolutely break down. (5)*

In Darwin's day, it was assumed that cells were very simple. In the last half of the 20th century, however, it has come to light that inside each living cell are vastly complex molecular machines made up of various protein parts. Organs, which are made up of these complex cells, have also been shown to be much more complex than previously believed.

The blueprints for assembling the protein parts for cells and organs in correct timing and order are encoded into our DNA, which is similar to binary computer code, although it is quaternary (having 4 letters instead of 2). The density of the information encoded into DNA staggers the imagination; there is enough information-storing space in a half-teaspoon of DNA to store all of the assembly instructions for every creature ever made, and room left over to include every book ever written!

In addition to the incredible information-storing capacity in DNA, there are machines and systems in biology which vastly exceed mankind's creative capacity in terms of their complexity. For example, the blood-clotting mechanism requires a sequence of 20 different proteins (each of which has an average chance of 1 in 8.03 x 10 to the 59th power of forming by random chance!) triggering one another like dominoes falling in order, until a fibrin mesh scaffolding is formed for the clot itself.

If you subtract any one single protein (regardless of where in the sequence of 20), this scaffolding fails to form, and no blood clot is possible. Without clotting, any creature with a circulatory system would bleed to death from a tiny wound, similarly to what happens to hemophiliacs.

Now think about how this compares to Darwin's criterion for his own theory. Macro-evolution requires a mutation for every step, each of which needs to confer an advantage in surviving or creating offspring to be retained by natural selection. Even if we grant the creation of proteins by random chance (which is extremely unlikely), at steps 1, 2 ,3, 4, etc. on up to and through step 19, there is no advantage conferred toward the production of a blood clot until step 20 is completed! If you reduce the complexity by any single component (regardless of where in the sequence the single component is), the system doesn't work, and has no reason to be retained by natural selection. This is Irreducible Complexity.

Let's look at another example. The Bacterial Flagellum is a tail-like protein propeller attached to one end of a bacterium that propels the organism through its environment via rapid rotations (like a miniature outboard motor driving a whip in circular motion). It has components that are remarkably similar to a man-made outboard motor, such as a rotor, a U-joint, a stator, a driveshaft, a propeller, bushings, and O-rings.

There are at least 40 different protein parts required for the assembly of a flagellum. Many of the flagellar proteins control the construction process, switching the building phases on and off with chemical triggers at just the right times, and setting up construction in the proper sequence. It is an engineering marvel. If you deduct 1% of the parts, you don't have a 99% functional bacterial flagellum; it becomes completely dysfunctional, and you have nothing but a hindrance (probably fatal) to any organism attached to it. The following picture hints at its complexity...

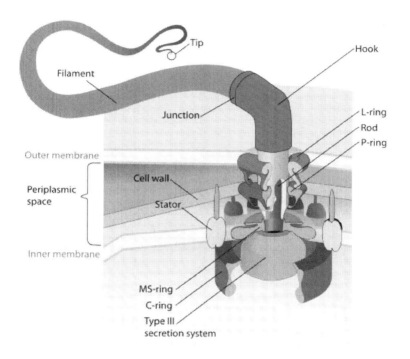

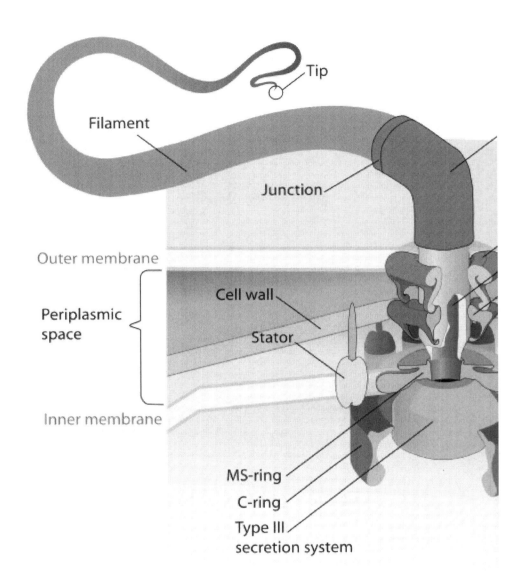

Tip

Filament

Junction

Outer membrane

Periplasmic space

Cell wall

Stator

Inner membrane

MS-ring

C-ring

Type III secretion system

Consider the fact that it is conservatively calculated that the odds of this incredible structure forming by random chance is 1 in 10 to the 1170th power. (6) According to probability theorists, anything with a chance lower than 1 in 10 to the 50th power is mathematically impossible, so it doesn't matter how much time you give it—it simply won't occur by chance alone.

Another incredible array of irreducibly complex structures are present in the wings of birds. If we imagine mutations happening one small increment at a time, think about the aeons of vulnerability proto-avians would have as they were supposedly evolving into birds with effective flight capability. I have no affiliation with, nor do I benefit from promoting Illustra Media, but their recent film *Genius: the Flight of Birds* illustrates what would be necessary for this process excellently and beautifully.

Another mind-boggling, irreducibly complex process in nature is that which is undergone by caterpillars (and other forms of larvae) in the chrysalis as they morph into beautiful, entirely different creatures like butterflies. As it happens they actually digest the vast majority of their bodies (all except certain cells called "imaginal disks"), and build an entirely new body structure within the chrysalis. Now taking into account the facts that: 1) evolutionary mutations must take place in the early (***pre***-chrysalis) stage to set up this mind-blowing process, and 2) sexual maturity and procreation don't occur until the ***post***-chrysalis stage, on the Darwinian view we have a dilemma! Mutations don't happen in bunches; they happen one at a time. As we covered previously, top mainstream scientists estimate that negative mutations outnumber positive ones by about a million to one. How on earth could a sufficient number of germline mutations to effect this orchestral metamorphosis accrue without the destruction of the creature millions of times over?! With a transcendent Designer, we can imagine it. On Darwinism, it's a pipe-dream which is so far-fetched that it (again) fails to pass the "laugh test". At the risk of sounding like a shill, I need to once again recommend an Illustra DVD called *Metamorphosis* which elucidates this incredible process beyond what I can describe here. I don't make any money from that, and I guarantee that you'll be blown away by it.

Going back to the flagellum, just recently, a vastly more complex gear-driven, seven-engine, magnetic-guided flagellar bundle was discovered. Here is an piece on it from www.evolutionnews.org:

Souped-Up Hyperdrive Flagellum Discovered

Evolution News & Views December 3, 2012 5:05 AM | Permalink

Get a load of this -- a bacterium that packs a gear-driven, seven-engine, magnetic-guided flagellar bundle that gets 0 to 300 micrometers in one second, ten times faster than *E. coli*.

If you thought the standard bacterial flagellum made the case for intelligent design, wait till you hear the specs on MO-1, a marine bacterium described by Japanese researchers in the*Proceedings of the National Academy of Sciences*. Edited by Howard Berg, Harvard's mastermind of flagellum reverse engineering, this paper describes the Ferrari of flagella.

Instead of being a simple helically wound propeller driven by a rotary motor, it is a complex organelle consisting of 7 flagella and 24 fibrils that form a tight bundle enveloped by a glycoprotein sheath.... the flagella of MO-1 must rotate individually, and yet the entire bundle functions as a unit to comprise a motility organelle.

To feel the Wow! factor, jump ahead to Figure 6 in the paper. It shows seven engines in one, arranged in a hexagonal array, stylized by the authors in a cross-sectional model that shows them all as gears interacting with 24 smaller gears between them. The flagella rotate one way, and the smaller gears rotate the opposite way to maximize torque while minimizing friction. Download the movie from the Supplemental Information page to see the gears in action.

Electron micrographs included in the paper show that the model is not unrealistic. These flagella really are tightly packed in a sheath, suggesting that the bundle acts like a gear-driven hyperdrive.

Here we have used electron cryotomography **to visualize the 3D architecture of the sheathed flagella**. The seven filaments are enveloped with 24 fibrils in the sheath, and their basal bodies are arranged in an intertwined hexagonal array similar to the thick and thin filaments of vertebrate skeletal muscles. **This complex and exquisite architecture** strongly suggests that the fibrils counter-rotate between flagella in direct contact **to minimize the friction of high-speed rotation** of individual flagella in the tight bundle within the sheath to enable MO-1 cells to swim at about 300 µm/s. (Emphasis added.)

At microbial level, that's more than 10 body lengths per second. The authors were clearly excited by this engine, sounding like young men checking out high-performance cars, talking thrust, gear ratios and torque.

MO-1 is a magnetotactic bacterium **capable of orienting its cell body along the geomagnetic**

field lines by using **magnetosomes**. The MO-1 cell has a flagellar apparatus with two lophotrichous [containing numerous flagella in] bundles. In contrast to peritrichously [flagella all over the cell] flagellated bacteria, MO-1 cells **swim constantly in a helical trajectory** toward magnetic north, **and the trajectory changes from right-handed to left-handed without changes in velocity or direction**. The cells are **able to swim as fast as 300 μm/s, which is nearly 10-fold faster** than *E. coli* and *Salmonella*. Although the flagella of the other types of bacteria usually work individually or by forming a loose bundle to produce thrust, the flagellar apparatus of MO-1 is **a tight bundle of seven flagella enveloped in a sheath** made of glycoproteins. **This unique architecture appears to be essential for the smooth and high-speed swimming of MO-1.**

They can't see actual gears, of course, but physics demands that the mechanism of rotation must have something like it:

We hypothesize that, whereas each of the seven flagella has its **torque-generating motor**, the 24 fibrils counter rotate between the flagellar filaments **to minimize the friction** that would be generated if the flagella were directly packed together in a tight bundle. **A schematic diagram representing our hypothesis is presented in Fig. 6.** The flagella are **represented as large brown gears and the fibrils are represented as small blue-green gears.** The flagella and fibrils rotate counterclockwise and clockwise, respectively, as indicated by the arrows, to minimize friction (Movie S1). Although there is no direct evidence that the fibrils can rotate freely in the opposite direction as the flagellar filaments with which they are in direct contact, **we think this is the simplest interpretation to explain the superior function afforded by the complex architecture** of the MO-1 flagellar apparatus.

Considering the **very tight packing** of the 7 flagella and 24 fibrils that **are in direct physical contact** within the sheath, **there appears to be no other way for the flagella to rotate at high speed without the counter rotation of the intervening fibrils.** Although the fibrils and the surrounding sheath are in direct contact, the friction between them would be small because of the stocking-like flexibility of the sheath. **This design must be playing an essential role in the fast, smooth rotation of the flagellar apparatus that allows the rapid swimming of MO-1.**

With powerful evidence of design like this, did the researchers become converts to intelligent design? We can't know, but would *PNAS* have printed such a paper without an obligatory tribute to unguided materialistic evolution? Evolution is not mentioned until the last paragraph:

Taken together, these features of the MO-1 flagellar apparatus represent **an advanced level of evolution of a motility apparatus.** It is also intriguing that the **same pattern of an intertwined hexagonal array in two evolutionary distant systems**: the basal bodies of flagella and fibrils of the MO-1 flagellar apparatus, and the thick and thin filaments in vertebrate skeletal muscle. **Similar architectures of filamentous structures presumably evolved independently** in prokaryotes and eukaryotes **to fulfill the requirements** for two very distinct **mechanisms to generate motion: counter rotation and axial sliding.**

OK, so the Darwinists got their offering, but it leaves a bad aftertaste: now, they have to believe that advanced mechanisms for generating motion evolved not just once, but twice -- completely independent of each other. Thanks a lot, guys. Wait till the intelligent-design movement hears about this.

Oops, too late.

(http://www.evolutionnews.org/2012/12/souped-up_flage066921.html).

"Tree of life"?

Now one might wonder: "But what about Darwin's 'tree of life'? Haven't we seen pictures of this showing a smooth continuum of the evolution of all major life forms from the last universal common ancestor?" Well, unfortunately, these 'tree of life' pictures represent art more than they represent science. Although these are frequently touted as proof of Darwinism, the transitional forms shown don't reflect creatures whose fossils have actually **been found**, but rather forms which **are expected to have existed** per the central dogma of Darwinism.

Read what a widely respected Biologist named Eugene Koonin (a Senior Investigator at the National Center for Biotechnology Information, National Library of Medicine, National Institutes of Health) wrote in a recent peer-reviewed paper:

> *Major transitions in biological evolution show the same pattern of sudden emergence of diverse forms at a new level of complexity. The relationships between major groups within an emergent new class of biological entities are hard to decipher and do not seem to fit the tree pattern that, following Darwin's original proposal, remains the dominant description of biological evolution. The cases in point include the origin of complex RNA molecules and protein folds; major groups of*

viruses; archaea and bacteria, and the principal lineages within each of these prokaryotic domains; eukaryotic supergroups; and animal phyla. In each of these pivotal nexuses in life's history, the principal "types" seem to appear rapidly and fully equipped with the signature features of the respective new level of biological organization. No intermediate "grades" or intermediate forms between different types are detectable. -- The Biological Big Bang model for the major transitions in evolution, 2007, Abstract.

Koonin goes on to provide what seems to me to be a lame rationalization of why these transitional forms are missing:

Usually, this pattern is attributed to cladogenesis compressed in time, combined with the inevitable erosion of the phylogenetic signal.

"Clades" (from which his term "cladogenesis" comes) are hypothesized "branches" in the supposed "Tree of Life". "Phylogenetic" means relationships to be discovered through molecular sequencing data. Yet why would these imagined transitional forms be more "compressed in time" or "eroded" than the rest of the forms, for which we have abundant fossils? To the contrary, transitional forms would be a veritable freak show of partially developed creatures with partially developed features. Since no mutation in the history of Biology has ever been shown to **add** information (yet most will degrade it), one would think there should be myriads of unsuccessful transitional forms! In all of these transitional stages, the partially finished features would tend to be a hindrance, if not downright fatal. Yet for some reason *"No intermediate 'grades' or intermediate forms between different types are detectable"* according to Koonin. With all due respect, this doesn't pass the laugh test. Once these hypothetical transitional forms are subtracted from the 'tree' illustrations, it no longer looks like a tree at all.

The reason these gaps are a problem is that it clashes with the Darwinian continuum narrative. Darwinism needs two things to succeed: 1) random mutations, and 2) natural selection ("survival of the fittest"). The second of these two is uncontroversial – we see the survival of the fittest demonstrated constantly in nature. The first, however -- which purportedly is responsible for the new features which can be retained by the second -- actually tends to create deleterious (harmful) mutations in far, far greater numbers than neutral or helpful mutations. The best estimates seem to be a ratio of about one good mutation (genetic drift or degradation that accidentally happens to benefit the creature) for every one million that are destructive (Gerrish and Lenski, 1998). This is an indescribably huge problem for Darwinism (or any materialistic theory). Since multiple, coordinated, mutations are necessary for any substantial change in a species, this catapults the improbability to far beyond the threshold of possibility (1 in 10 to the

50th power). If we ignore this, though, we would expect to find a smooth continuum connecting all forms of life, as steady progress is far more likely than rapid change. Unfortunately for the materialist, however, that's not what we find.

Convergence

Another feature of life that makes no sense from a materialist perspective is the recurrence of startling similarities in biologically unrelated forms of life. "Convergence" refers to the same features showing up in unrelated creatures, despite the possibility of myriad choices of evolutionary "pathways" which presumably could be (or could have been) taken. There is no known force which would constrain all of these wildly diverse pathways into the same ending, yet there they are. Since Darwinism is thought to be a "contingent" (non-restricted) process, -- i.e. it shouldn't tend to go the same way twice -- this has puzzled inquiring minds. Many respected biologists (like the late Stephen Jay Gould, and Simon Conway-Morris) have noted that it's bizarre that unguided Darwinian evolution would ever have gone down the same mutational paths more than once, or arrived at the same structure more than once, in unrelated creatures. As a metaphor, imagine asking several separate groups of people to each create a long, complicated equation over the course of sixty years by adding, subtracting, multiplying and dividing random numbers, eventually arriving at a final number. At the end of the sixty years, when you check the numbers, you find that all the groups' equations resulted in the exact same number! There are literally dozens of purportedly contingent, yet matching results of Darwinian processes in nature, all far, far more unlikely than the number metaphor above.

Paleontologist J. William Schopf, one of the world's leading authorities on early life on Earth, had made the following prediction in the book *Life's Origin* (anticipating that a cause for convergence would be found at the biochemical level):

Because biochemical systems comprise many intricately interlinked pieces, any particular full-blown system can only arise once...Since any complete biochemical system is far too elaborate to have evolved more than once in the history of life, it is safe to assume that microbes of the primal LCA cell line ["LCA" stands for "Last Common Ancestor"] *had the same traits that characterize all its present-day descendents.*

But this prediction has now been eviscerated by more advanced biochemical studies, which show no such traits. As Biochemist Dr. Fazale Rana observes, "This pattern, expected by Schopf and other evolutionary biologists, is simply not observed at the biochemical level" (www.reasons.org).

Just a few of the many complex biological features without a molecular connection to a common ancestor are the wings of birds and bats, the strikingly similar (yet unrelated) limb structures of bats and flying lemurs, seven distinct structures in the forebrain of parrots, songbirds, and hummingbirds (which structures are genetically unrelated), echolocation in two types of bats: microchiroptera and megachiroptera (the structures of which are genetically unrelated), the eye structure of the cephalopods (nautili, cuttlefish, squids, and octopods) and those of vertebrates, the eye structures and some hunting tactics of the sandlance fish and the chameleon lizard, toothed and baleen whales' ability to dive deep into the ocean (which are genetically separate), and dozens of other examples. Dr. Rana has a list of over one hundred examples in his book *The Cell's Design*. This has been a real head-scratcher for committed Darwinists, but for those with minds open to an Intelligent Designer, it makes more sense. Designers are free to use their designs for more than one application.

Going back to our previous subject, what if we just ignored the previously mentioned problems of forming the first cell, and assume that we're starting the Darwinian process from the bacterial level and advancing to the human level? On page 153 of the book *Who Was Adam?*, Fazale Rana and Hugh Ross cite one of the world's most prominent evolutionists, Dr. Francisco Ayala of UC

Irvine, as calculating the minimal odds of human beings evolving from the bacterial level to be 1 in 10 to the 1 millionth power. Three physicists, John Barrow, Brandon Carter and Frank Tipler, did roughly the same calculation but included some important factors that Ayala overlooked, and came up with the number 1 in 10 to the 24 millionth power. Keep in mind that Tipler is Professor of Mathematical Physics at Tulane University, and is well-versed in calculating collective probabilities.

Given the odds, in the time that would pass before any of these things would happen, our sun would have ceased to be a main sequence star and incinerated the earth (the path that it is currently on)

Some of the extremely unlikely steps in the purported evolution of Homo Sapiens are the following (from Barrow and Tipler's book *The Anthropic Cosmological Principle*, pp. 562-564).

1. The development of the DNA-based genetic

    code.

2. The invention of aerobic respiration.

3. The invention of glucose fermentation to pyruvic acid.

4. The origin of autotropic photosynthesis. [This trait may well not be in the human lineage but it seems necessary for human evolution and that is sufficient.]

5. The origin of mitochondria.

6. The formation of the cenriole/kinetosome/undilipodia complex. [The microtubules which make up this complex have a dual use: they are used to separate the chromosomes during cell division in eukaryotes and to form the axons and dendrites of nerve cells.]

7. The evolution of an eye precursor. [I remarked earlier that the eye has evolved over forty times, but there is some evidence suggesting that these all developed from an eye precursor that itself only evolved once.]

8. The development of endoskeleton.

9. The development of chordates.

10. The development of *Homo sapiens* in the chordate lineage.

Again, according to probability theorists, any event with lower odds than 1 in 10 to the 50th power is mathematically impossible. Therefore unguided Darwinian evolution is mathematically impossible!

Reduced to a propositional argument, it might go like this:

Biological "Hardware" (Complex Structure) Argument

1. According to leading Darwinists, odds of humans evolving from a single-celled creature are 1 in $10^{24,000,000}$.

2. According to probability theorists, anything with lower odds than 1 in 10^{50} is mathematically impossible.

3. Therefore, Darwinian evolution of human beings is mathematically impossible.

Now, these two sets of odds (totaling to 1 in $10^{363,999,866}$) seem overwhelming to say the least; why would scientists insist that creations like these could have come about by evolution? To re-iterate, it seems that biological science has become dominated by atheistic philosophers. Science is "a search for truth", but the oligarchy in control in this day and age is trying to change that to "a search for truth by naturalistic (atheistic) means". To them, the idea of God is unacceptable, so science cannot consider even the possibility that God created this universe and all that is in it. Some people simply don't want rules (even a set of reasonable, light, quality-of-life-enhancing rules) of any sort. Consider this quote by Thomas Nagel:

> *I want atheism to be true and am made uneasy by the fact that some of the most intelligent and well-informed people I know are religious believers. It isn't just that I don't believe in God and, naturally, hope that I'm right in my belief. It's that I hope there is no God! I don't want there to be a God; I don't want the universe to be like that. [The Last Word" by Thomas Nagel, Oxford University Press: 1997].*

Another example of "selective reasoning" came courtesy of Harvard Neurobiologist George Wald:

One has only to contemplate the magnitude of this task to concede that the spontaneous generation of a living organism is impossible. Yet here we are -- as a result, I believe, of spontaneous generation.

To be fair, Wald eventually became an Intelligent Design advocate.

The above quotes are textbook examples of bias. Yet it gets worse. Take a look at the following quote by prominent Darwinist Richard Lewontin, and consider whether his viewpoint is logically sound. Unfortunately, this quote seems to be representative of how many Darwinists think, and how they want everyone else to think:

Our willingness to accept scientific claims that are against common sense is the key to an understanding of the real struggle between science and the supernatural. We take the side of science in spite of the patent absurdity of some of its constructs, in spite of its failure to fulfill many of its extravagant promises of health and life, in spite of the tolerance of the scientific community for unsubstantiated just-so stories, because we have a prior commitment, a commitment to materialism. It is not that the methods and institutions of science somehow compel us to accept a material explanation of the phenomenal world, but, on the contrary, that we are forced by our a priori adherence to material causes to create an apparatus of investigation and a set of concepts that produce material explanations, no matter how counter-intuitive, no matter how mystifying to the uninitiated. Moreover, that materialism is absolute, for we cannot allow a Divine Foot in the door. (7)

One wonders why such a concerted effort is made to deny the metaphysical into the pool of live options. Perhaps the following quote by another prominent Darwinist named Aldous Huxley provides some insight:

> *I had motives for not wanting the world to have meaning; consequently assumed that it had none, and was able without any difficulty to find satisfying reasons for this assumption ... For myself, as no doubt, for most of my contemporaries, the philosophy of meaninglessness was essentially an instrument of liberation. The liberation we desired was simultaneous liberation from a certain political and economic system, and liberation from a certain system of morality. We objected to the morality because it interfered with our sexual freedom. (8)*

Now, just for fun, look at the following Bible passage, and think about how it relates to the quotes above:

> *For since the creation of the world His invisible attributes, His eternal power and divine nature, have been clearly seen, being understood through what has been made, so that they are without excuse.*
> *For even though they knew God, they did not honor Him as God or give thanks, but they became futile in their speculations, and their foolish heart was darkened. Professing to be wise, they became fools. --Romans 1:20-22.*

Perhaps this is a good place to ponder a quote from Nobel-Prize winning organic chemist Christian de Duve:

> *If you equate the probability of the birth of a bacteria cell to chance*

assembly of its atoms, eternity will not suffice to produce one... Faced with the enormous sum of lucky draws behind the success of the evolutionary game, one may legitimately wonder to what extent this success is actually written into the fabric of the universe. (9)

God has indeed left His signature in nature in its irreducible complexity and fine-tuning. Darwinism has failed repeatedly when tested as an explanation for the existence of life. Thousands of scientists have recognized this (including Nobel Prize-winners like Brian Josephson, Richard Smalley, Abdus Salam, Sir Jon Eccles, Ernst Boris Chain, Wolgang Pauli and Guglielmo Marconi - http://www.uncommondescent.com/intelligent-design/seven-nobel-laureates-in-science-who-either-supported-intelligent-design-or-attacked-darwinian-evolution/). Over eight hundred have signed a document called the "Dissent from Darwinism" (http://www.dissentfromdarwin.org/) to express their disagreement with philosophical naturalism dominating science through Darwinism (and far more would sign it if it weren't for the threat that would entail for their careers). We simply need to "have eyes to see, and ears to hear", and to stop listening to atheistic philosophers disguised as scientists, who try to insist that the supernatural or metaphysical is off-limits for science. "Reasonable faith" is going in the same direction to which the evidence is pointing. The teachings of the Bible, understood properly, merge perfectly with science.

CHAPTER FOUR: THE SOFTWARE OF LIFE ARGUMENT

"There's a sign on the wall
But she wants to be sure
'cause you know sometimes words have two
meanings."

~from *"Stairway to Heaven"*, by Led Zeppelin

Image from *Elephants Not Included Lending Library*

The finest assembly of computer hardware will avail you nothing without software. Many of us don't fully appreciate this, as nearly all computers come pre-loaded with software ("guilty!"). But nevertheless, without "software" (programming), any kind of "hardware" is useless. Software is tantamount to information. As I mentioned in the previous chapter, the blueprints for assembling the protein parts for cells and organs in correct timing and order are encoded into our DNA, which is similar to binary computer code, although it is quaternary (having 4 letters instead of 2). This is the "software" or programming that allows for life to exist. It contains a substantial amount of the blueprint information for biological structures and forms. Other "blueprint" components which are encoded elsewhere in cells interact with it. This requires a "language convention" with which these components can interact, and each message must be interpreted properly to allow for that.

The density of the information encoded into DNA staggers the imagination; there is enough information-storing space in a half-teaspoon of DNA to store all of the assembly instructions for every creature ever made, and room left over to include every book ever written! The information content of a bacterium has been estimated to be around 10,000,000,000,000 bits of information -- comparable to a hundred million pages of Encyclopaedia Britannica. (1) Even if the insurmountable problems with the structure of life's "hardware" assembly mentioned in the last chapter were somehow abridged, another completely separate phenomenon is needed for this life to operate and reproduce—a DNA language!

The information stored in life's DNA is encoded by way various arrangements of four molecules called nucleotides; adenine, guanine, cytosine and thymine. These molecules are arranged in chains bonded together into what is called a "double helix", which looks like a ladder that has been twisted into a corkscrew shape.

Just as with binary computer code, this seemingly simple structure can store vast amounts of information for the assembly of proteins throughout the organism. If all the DNA info in the one human body were printed in books, it would be enough to fill the Grand Canyon fifty times over! Moreover, the information would be nothing but gibberish, and would be worthless for constructing proteins unless there was an established language convention to which it conformed. This raises the question "who established the language convention?"

As mind-boggling as this seems so far, it gets even better. The instructions for creating DNA are encoded into proteins! This raises the question, "which came first; the DNA or the proteins?!" We have seen clear evidence in the last chapter that neither proteins nor DNA could be expected to arise spontaneously, but here we see that problem multiplied exponentially.

If life arose by random chance, among other things, we would have to have:

1) amino acids assembling spontaneously, in the correct order -- following a specific, very complex language convention -- to effect the assembly of proteins, with the correct chirality (all "left-handed" molecules),

2) proteins assembling spontaneously in the correct order -- following a specific, very complex language convention -- to regulate the construction and assembly of DNA, and

3) nucleic acids assembling spontaneously to create DNA simultaneously with the arisal of proteins, and with the correct chirality ("right-handedness"), in the correct order, and following the same, very specific complex language convention in order to orchestrate the assembly of proteins!

One is tempted to ask the question "what came first, the chicken (proteins) or the egg (DNA)?", but in this case, both phenomena would have to arise simultaneously and following the same language convention, or they would both be completely useless.

As Nobel Prize-winning biochemist Jacques Monod put it:

The major problem is the origin of the genetic code and of its translation mechanism. Indeed, instead of a problem it ought rather to be called a riddle. The code is meaningless unless translated. The modern cell's translating machinery consists of at least fifty macromolecular components which are themselves coded in DNA: the code cannot be translated otherwise than by products of translation. It is the modern expression of omne vivum ex ovo [everything that lives, (comes) from an egg]. When and how did this circle become closed? It is exceedingly difficult to imagine. (2)

Monod is not the only Nobel-Prize winning scientist to cast doubt on a naturalistic explanation for life. Consider the words of Ilya Prigogine, a Chemist-Physicist and recipient of two Nobel Prizes in chemistry:

> *The statistical probability that organic structures and the most precisely harmonized reactions that typify living organisms would be generated by accident, is zero. (3)*

Now keep in mind that the conditions mentioned above are necessary, but are not sufficient for the creation of life. There are many, many more necessary components for DNA-based life. There are more challenges for the theory of spontaneous generation of life than we have room to discuss here, and this can be quickly confirmed by a survey of current theories, which encompass a huge array of approaches having one thing in common: none provide a plausible, detailed theory.

According to Doug Axe of Oxford University, the odds against just a minimal set of the *required proteins alone* to create simplest conceivable cell is 1 in $10^{41,000}$. So in addition to the improbabilities calculated in the last chapter, we can add an additional layer. The argument would look something like this:

Biological "Software" (Genetic Information) Argument

1. The odds of the genetic information required to make the proteins for a minimally complex single-celled creature arising by chance are 1 in $10^{41,000}$.

2. According to probability theorists, anything with lower odds than 1 in 10^{50} is mathematically impossible.

3. Therefore, a single-celled creature arising by chance is mathematically impossible.

Our collective improbability is now at least 1 in $10^{364,040,866}$. Suffice it to say that it takes more faith to believe this vast array of necessary conditions could coincidentally occur by chance than to believe in a transcendent Creator who has orchestrated it.

Modern science is now consistently revealing new, mindboggling features of the cellular world on a surprisingly regular basis. The "nanotechnology" that we observe functioning at this incredibly tiny level is overshadowed only by the immense complexity of the language and encoding which orchestrates it, and is built into it. I'll let Dr. Don E. Johnson sum it up:

> *Information is something that is useful that you can use to make predictions that have meaning, and the only way to get that is by intelligence. There is absolutely no way that ever has been shown to produce information other than by intelligence. And therefore, you have life, you have the complexity of the*

DNA structure and the amount of information that it contains, which is something that boggles very intelligent people. It makes absolutely zero sense to say it happened by chance. Things **had** **to** *have been intelligently designed, they* **could** **not** *have happened by chance.'* (Scienceintegrity.net. Dr. Don E. Johnson has two earned PhD's; one in Chemistry and one in Computer Science and Information Theory).

Forgive me for being redundant, but this is probably a good time to flash back on what we learned in the last chapter (because it applies to this chapter as well) - your body has literally hundreds of quadrillions of computers in it, some operating with triple layers of encryption! Also:

- the genetic system IS a pre-existing *operating system*;
- the specific *genetic program* (genome) is an application;

- the *native language* has a *codon-based encryption system*;
- the codes are *read* by *enzyme computers* with their own *operating system*;
- each enzyme's output is to *another operating system* in a ribosome;
- codes are *decrypted* and output to *tRNA computers*;
- each *codon-specified* amino acid is transported to a protein construction site; and
- in each cell, there are *multiple operating systems, multiple programming languages, encoding/decoding hardware and software, specialized communications systems, error detection/correction systems, specialized input/output* for organelle control and feedback, and a variety of *specialized "devices"* to accomplish the tasks of life. (Dr. Donald E. Johnson – who has earned PhD's in Chemistry and Computer Science -- via Uncommon Descent).

As astonishing as this is, there's more. There are overlapping codes, and codes within codes within codes (three layers of encryption). Some codes extend epigenetically (beyond the genes), and some rely on combinations of genes being switched on and off. Consider this quote in New Scientist:

> *A single gene can potentially code for tens of thousands of different proteins... It's the way in which genes are switched on and off, though, that has turned out to be really mind-boggling, with layer after layer of complexity emerging. (~Le Page, "Genome at 10," New Scientist, 6/16/10).*

Arguably the most prominent atheist of the 20th century, Antony Flew (Professor of Philosophy, author, and debater) announced in 2004 that he had become convinced that there is no way these things could have evolved by chance, due to their stunning information content. As he put it:

> *It now seems to me that the findings of more than fifty years of DNA research have provided materials for*

a new and enormously powerful argument to design. (4)

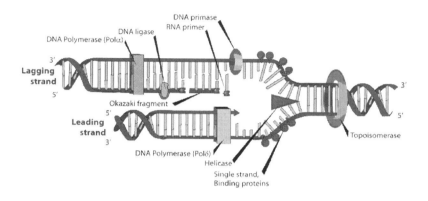

An artist's rendition of a moment of DNA replication (wordsandunwords.com).

In a bit of news breaking just recently, a joint scientific project called "ENCODE" has determined that a staggering 80% of what was previously considered "junk" DNA actually has purpose. From a materialist viewpoint, this increase in specified complexity dramatically increases the difficulty of arguing against an Intelligent Designer. Here Dr. Fazale Rana of RTB discusses the implications:

The Big Play

Shortly after the draft sequence of the human genome was published, researchers' initial estimates determined that only 1 percent of the human genome consisted of functional sequences, with the rest categorized as junk. But now the ENCODE team reports that a staggering 80 percent of the human genome consists of functional elements; and with the third phase of the project underway, that number may well increase.

The ENCODE project's impact will be far reaching, providing important knowledge about human biology and the etiology of genetic disorders, and guiding the future direction for biomedicine. The ENCODE results also influence the creation/evolution controversy.

Many skeptics and evolutionary biologists claim that the most compelling evidence for human evolution—and, thus, most potent challenge against intelligent design/creationism—is the human genome's vast amount of junk DNA. And yet, with the results of the ENCODE project, these arguments evaporate. The ENCODE project has radically altered our view of the human genome. It can no longer be considered a vast wasteland of junk, but must be seen as an elegant system that displays sophistication in its architecture and operation, far beyond what most evolutionary biologists ever imagined.

Called Back

Yet, just as creationists and ID proponents were celebrating this victory, some skeptics threw down the red flag, challenging the call on the field. They asserted that the results of the ENCODE project have been overhyped by the media and misconstrued by creationists and intelligent design (ID) adherents. It looked like the play was going to be called back.[2]

Specifically, the ENCODE "skeptics" claim:

The results of the project have been sensationalized and poorly reported by science journalists.

The discussion of the ENCODE results ignores the fact that nearly 50 percent of the human genome consists of transposable elements and two percent is comprised of pseudogenes, both of which are nonfunctional, junk sequences.

The ENCODE scientists detected biochemical activity for 80 percent of the human genome, but it is incorrect to equate biochemical activity with function.

The Play Stands

However, after careful review, it looks as if the play on the field stands. First off, it's hard to accept the claim that the popular science reports are hype.

The science journalists who reported on the ENCODE results are among the best in the world—and all it takes is a little digging to show that they reported the story accurately. For example, the ENCODE Project Consortium writes in the abstract of the summary/overview article published in Nature (September 6, 2012), "These data enabled us to assign biochemical functions for 80% of the genome, in particular outside the well-studied protein-coding regions."[3]

On September 5, ScienceDaily published a news item based on a press release issued by NIH/National Human Genome Institute (NHGRI), in which Eric D. Green, director of NHGRI, is quoted as saying,[4]

"During the early debates about the Human Genome Project, researchers had predicted that only a few percent of the human genome sequence encoded proteins, the workhorses of the cell, and the rest was junk. We now know that this conclusion was wrong."

When it comes to transposable elements and pseudogenes in the human genome, it is highly likely that the 80 percent of the human genome that possesses functional elements overlaps the 50 percent comprised of transposable elements and pseudogenes. A plethora of work indicates that both types of "junk" DNA are actually functional.[5] The functional DNA elements identified by the ENCODE project are involved in regulating gene expression. It is interesting to note that one of the functional roles of transposable elements and pseudogenes in the human genome relates to gene regulation.

Skeptics' final protest—the claim that biochemical activity doesn't equate to function—is a distinction without a difference, at least when it comes to the ENCODE study. In other words, the final protest fumbles. In some instances, it is true that biochemicalactivity doesn't equate to biochemical function. But it is hard to argue that this is the case for the ENCODE project. The project's investigators carefully and specifically chose assays to detect biochemical activity (transcription, binding of transcription factors, histone binding, sites where modified histones bind, methylation, and three-dimensional interactions between enhancers and genes) with well-established function. Biochemists have known for some time that the biochemical activities cataloged by the ENCODE Consortium are important for gene regulation and gene expression.

It seems that the distinction between biochemical activity and function is a "sleight of hand"—a ploy to detract from what Christian apologists are saying about the significance of ENCODE. The results of the ENCODE project are a "touchdown!" for creationists and ID adherents who have long argued that scientific advance will reveal that so-called junk DNA sequences are functional and, thus, evidence for design.

Source:
http://www.reasons.org/articles/responding-to-encode-skeptics

The Cambrian Explosion

About 540 million years ago, most of the body types in nature appeared suddenly in the fossil record without transitional forms preceding them. Since this is within the Cambrian period, and is the "Big Bang" of biology, it's called "The Cambrian Explosion". Charles Darwin, in his day, was very puzzled by it, but he thought that future digs would eventually discover these forms. He was wrong.

Paleontologists and others have now dug in every region of the earth, and have found no transitional forms which preceded the Cambrian. This sudden appearance of a massive new influx of complex information has puzzled scientists who are committed to the Darwinian paradigm. Richard Dawkins for example, stated the following in response to this puzzle: "It's as though they were just planted there, without any evolutionary history" (The Blind Watchmaker, p. 229).

Some scientists had proposed that maybe the precedent forms were soft-bodied, and therefore couldn't fossilize, but this hypothesis was blown out of the water when large quantities of sponge embryo fossils were discovered. It doesn't get much softer than sponge embryos, so Darwinists are stuck with the puzzle.

Speaking of transitional forms, as I mentioned before, there is a jaw-dropping *lack* of them between types of creatures as well. People think the fossil record is solid and complete because Darwinists constantly create and present hypothetical "trees of life" as if they are common knowledge. The truth of the matter is that these pictures represent a tiny amount of actual fossils, and a vast abundance of imaginative speculation. One of the world's most respected Darwinists, the late Stephen Jay Gould, once remarked:

"All paleontologists know that the fossil record contains precious little in the way of intermediate forms; transitions between major groups are characteristically abrupt", and *"The extreme rarity of transitional forms in the fossil record contains precious little in the way of intermediate forms;*

transitions between major groups are characteristically abrupt." (Gould, Stephen J., The Panda's Thumb, 1980, p. 189), and *"The extreme rarity of transitional forms in the fossil record persists as the trade secret of paleontology...the evolutionary trees that adorn our textbooks have data only at the tips and nodes of their branches; the rest is inference, however reasonable, not the evidence of fossils."* (Evolution's erratic pace, *Natural History, Vol. LXXXVI[5], May, 1977, p. 14).*

The problem with this standpoint is that bad mutations outnumber good mutations by such a staggering ratio. If the Darwinian paradigm were true, the earth would be littered with not just transitional forms, but a cornucopia of sad mutations which didn't live long. The fact that it is not speaks volumes.

Molecular Sequencing

An additional problem with the Darwinian paradigm that is related to the above, is the problem with molecular sequencing. "Molecular sequences" are molecular signatures of genes and proteins within cells that reflect the evolutionary path they took (if any). Since the 1990's, scientists have been able to map these sequences, and they completely clash with the "tree of life" paradigm. A recent cover story in the journal *New Scientist* called "Why Darwin was wrong about the tree of life" expressed it this way:

For a long time the holy grail was to build a tree of life," says Eric Bapteste, an evolutionary biologist at the Pierre and Marie Curie University in Paris, France. A few years ago it looked as though the grail was within reach. **But today the project lies in tatters, torn to pieces by an onslaught of negative evidence. Many biologists now argue that the tree concept is obsolete and needs to be discarded. "We have no evidence at all that the tree of life is a reality,"** *says Bapteste. That bombshell has*

*even persuaded some that our fundamental
view of biology needs to change. (*Graham
Lawton, *"Why Darwin was wrong about the
tree of life,"* New Scientist *[January 21,
2009] [emphasis added]*.

Who'da thunk it? Although the massive additional
improbability that this adds to the equation hasn't
yet been calculated, it is obviously going to
increase it manyfold.

Relevant quote:

*The complexity of biology has seemed
to grow by orders of magnitude.
Biology's new glimpse at a universe of
non-coding DNA — what used to be
called 'junk' DNA — has been
fascinating and befuddling...the
signaling information in cells is
organized through networks of
information rather than simple
discrete pathways. It's infinitely more
complex."*-- Erika Hayden, "Life is

Complicated," Nature, 3/31/10, p. 664-667

So are we allowed to infer "design" from the complexities explored hereto? I certainly think we can. Many people not only don't know these things, but assume that since Science has generally not inferred design, that it must be because there is no evidence for it. In many cases, they have not considered that some Scientists may be operating under the influence of ulterior motives. Additionally, they have no idea that many scientists are horrendous philosophers, and don't even notice the prevailing mistake of drifting from Methodological Materialism (the presumption in Science that supernatural causes are not to be considered) to Philosophical Materialism (the idea that therefore the supernatural cannot possibly exist).

That being said, I would be remiss if I didn't mention that I think Psychological and Sociological factors are in play here. Human Beings have a tendency to conform, so as not to be "left out" or ostracized. "Groupthink" is a powerful force.

Three major "authorities" to which people generally conform are peers, the media, and academia. But just as with computers, if you have errors which have crept into the "code" (or the "conventional wisdom" of the popular "groupthink"), you will arrive at erroneous conclusions. The computing term for this is "garbage in, garbage out". Unfortunately many in the "top tier" of these three groups have suffered an incremental drift to the left, which was deliberately instigated over a long period of time by European Marxists' avowed "Long March Through The Institutions" (for more on this, see: The Fabian Socialists and The Frankfurt School). It seems to me that the temptation to overturn one of the pillars of Western Civilization (Theism) on a continent (Europe) which had witnessed centuries of entanglement, corruption and collusion between church and state was the primary motivating factor in Darwinism's theory becoming popular so quickly there. The U.S.A. was a much harder sell – easy to imagine because in addition to Theistic Evolution being a conceivable rendering of Genesis 1, there are about fifty other arguments for God's existence – but they kept at it tenaciously over the past 150 years.

Unfortunately, many in America get "a tingle up their leg" over European accents, which I fear has been a far greater influence than any reasoning they had to offer. Yet over time, the cultural inertia grew, and it became fashionable for the control freaks at Universities and in the media (many of whom are simply trying to *sound* smart, and are regurgitating what they believe to be "conventional wisdom" in academia without fully understanding it) to insist that Darwinism is "the only **_modern_** biological worldview". This has had a perverse influence on "low-information voters" in the culture (whom, as you probably know if you watch the news, often behave like animals after being immersed in that presumption for years).

Yet ironically, atheism is actually still <u>not</u> the prevailing metaphysical view among American Scientists. Perhaps due to lack of a state church, we have less frustration with the powers-that-be on that level. According to a recent Pew poll, less than half of The AAAS (The American Association for the Advancement of Science; the world's largest general scientific society) are atheists (http://www.pewforum.org/2009/11/05/scientists-and-belief/), so this is a false narrative being peddled by a pushy oligarchy which feels a need to "control the agenda". In fact, only 17% of those Scientists identified themselves as atheists! While it's true that many of these Scientists are Theistic Evolutionists, many of them don't seem to understand that the reason Darwinism got traction in the first place is because it was seen as a lever with which to dislodge God from culture. When Richard Dawkins made the following quote, for example, he was echoing decades of elitists' attempts to rid the earth of Theism: "Although atheism might have been logically tenable before Charles Darwin, Darwin made it possible to be an intellectually fulfilled atheist." [*The Blind Watchmaker*, p. 6].

The fact that the likes of Richard Dawkins think it should actually be made illegal to teach evidence-based Intelligent Design should not be missed or ignored. The rights spoken of by America's founders were seen to be "inalienable" because they were secured by Nature's God; The Creator. In order to "alienate" these Natural Laws, tyrants must first convince people that God doesn't exist.

I think it's high time these intellectual fascists got some stronger resistance from those timid rank and file scientists who have not yet signed the "Dissent from Darwinism" document, and are otherwise silent. Silence is presumed to be assent in this case, and terrible philosophy like Philosophical-Materialism-As-A-Spinoff-From-Methodological-Methodological-Materialism is something to which thinking people should not assent. It's amusing that many of these same atheists will bray about "hegemony" when criticizing things like Western Civilization, but they engage in brazen and amateurish cultural hegemony when it comes to metaphysics.

Going back to hard Science, another one of the problems that Darwinism must solve (ha ha) is summed up very well by biophysicist, Hubert Yockey. The "problem" is that the genetic code has error-minimization abilities built into it that are astonishing. The particular question addressed in his book *Information Theory and Molecular Biology* is: "If the genetic code could change over time to yield a set of rules that allowed for the best possible error-minimization capacity, then is there enough time for this process to occur?" Yockey determined that natural selection would have to explore 1.4 x 10 to the 70th power (1.4 followed by 70 zeros, a very, very large number!) different genetic codes to discover the universal genetic code found in nature. The maximum time available for it to organize the universal code-of-life was estimated 6.3 x 10 to the 15th power seconds or 200 million years. Darwinian processes would have to evaluate roughly 10 to the 55th power ***codes-per-second*** in the available time to find the one that's universal. Put simply, Darwinism lacks the time necessary to find the universal genetic code by many billions of trillions of years (literally).

On *top* of this, as if to kick a dead theory when it's down, Nobel Laureate (and co-discoverer of DNA) Francis Crick argued that the genetic code can't evolve in any substantial way, because if the rules of the code were altered in any direction, it would result in a catastrophic condition for the cell. Can you say "intractable problem"?

So what do the super-intelligent say about all this? I did a little bit of research on the highest IQ's on earth, and to my surprise found indications that four out of the top five were not atheists. The man who may be the smartest of them all – Christopher Langan (IQ around 200) – is an unabashed Intelligent Design proponent. He had a piece in William Dembski's ID essay book *Uncommon Dissent* which was called *Cheating the Millenium: The Mounting Explanatory Debts of Scientific Naturalism.* Langan explains on his website that he believes "since Biblical accounts of the genesis of our world and species are true but metaphorical, our task is to correctly decipher the metaphor in light of scientific evidence also given to us by God".

Langan has a "theory of everything" (which I've read, but don't fully understand) called *The Cognitive-Theoretic Model of The Universe* (CTMU). In his words, it:

...attempts to explain the connection between mind and reality, and therefore the presence of cognition and universe in the same phrase. In explaining this relationship, the CTMU shows that reality possesses a complex property akin to self-awareness. That is, just as the mind is real, reality is in some respects like a mind. But when we attempt to answer the obvious question "whose mind?", the answer turns out to be a mathematical and scientific definition of God. This implies that we all exist in what can be called "the Mind of God", and that our individual minds are parts of God's Mind. They are not as powerful as God's Mind, for they are only parts thereof; yet, they are directly connected to the greatest source of knowledge and power that exists. This connection of our minds to the Mind of God, which is like the connection of parts to a whole, is what we sometimes call the soul or spirit, and it is the most crucial and

essential part of being human. (CTMU.org).

Again, I don't necessarily endorse all of his beliefs, but that's not the point. The point is that some **_VERY_** smart people have not accepted atheism, including most scientists, and they have good reason for not doing so. In popular culture, the opposite impression has developed, so more work needs to be done here in the name of intellectual integrity. If you are a truth-seeker, and find it disappointing when culture gloms on to an ungrounded myth (like neo-Darwinism), please share this information.

I'll wrap this chapter up with an interesting image. The following is what a gene regulatory network looks like for a tissue type called endomesoderm, in simple sea urchins. Does this look like a series of accidents to you, or does it look like design?

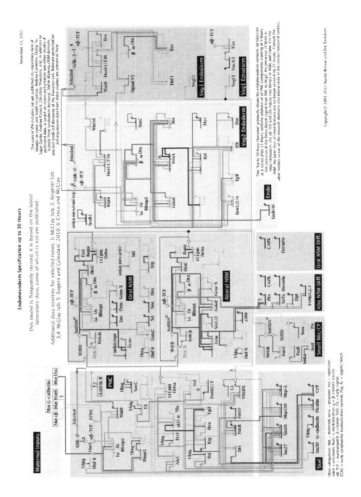

Endomesoderm Specification up to 30 Hours

This model is frequently revised. It is based on the latest laboratory data, some of which is not yet published.

Additional data sources for selected notes: 1: McClay lab; 2: Angerer lab; 3,4 McClay lab; 5: Rogers and Calestani 2010; 6: Croce and McClay

November 21, 2011

The current tPA includes not yet published cis-regulatory data of Smadi/Lin sem, 2nd Smith/Lin plexa), Andrew Cameron, Qiang Tu, Sagar Damle, Andrew Ransick, Christina Theodoris, and, in addition to published data, is based on current perturbation and other results of Isabelle Peter endoderm domain), Joel McManus HOM domain), and Joel Smith JCP divisions of the Davidson Lab. Relevant perturbation and expression data from these studies are presented here.

Maternal Inputs

Copyright © 2001-2011 Hamid Bolouri and Eric Davidson

CHAPTER FIVE: THE NOOLOGICAL (EXISTENCE OF MIND) ARGUMENT

"*Images of broken light which dance before me like a million eyes,*
That call me on and on across the universe,
Thoughts meander like a restless wind inside a letter box they
Tumble blindly as they make their way
Across the universe."

~from *Across the Universe*, by the Beatles

W. A. MOZART

Rondo Alla Turca
Turkish March

Have you ever wondered to yourself, "Where do my thoughts come from?" Or maybe, "why do I care about, or wonder about where my thoughts come from?" Darwinian evolutionists claim that we are nothing but particles of matter in a specific arrangement, but the self-awareness and consciousness of our minds provide prima facie ("on its first appearance") evidence that we consist of much more than that. How could human minds result from the mere re-arrangement of brute matter? It is much easier to see how a Transcendent Being with a mind could produce the finite conscious minds that we possess.

Self-awareness itself is subjective evidence that we are more than simply highly evolved matter. If we were nothing but evolved matter, we would be simply "machines made of meat"—biological computers. It's easy to imagine robots or automatons that are programmed to perpetuate themselves (like the computer HAL 9000 in the movie 2001: A Space Odyssey), and which toward that end will claim to have self-awareness, yet which in actuality have no self-awareness.

Science fiction is full of imaginary creatures of this sort; programmed to claim human attributes such as self-awareness, yet actually being nothing but machines. This hypothetical creature that we could imagine is much simpler than a creature that is actually truly self-aware. If Darwinian evolution has occurred, it follows that the first (simplest) product would be a hypothetical creature of this variety (that is to say, an automaton), and not something much more complex which actually has self-awareness. If we were products of that process, we would not be self-aware, yet somehow here we are able to contemplate God's existence and our own existence.

To paraphrase Intelligent Design advocate Phil Johnson, given the fact that we have consciousness and self-awareness, what view of the universe makes more sense: the Biblical viewpoint that "In the beginning was the Divine Mind" (John 1:1), or the naturalistic viewpoint that "in the beginning were the particles"?

Michelangelo: The Creation of Adam

Think about the mental states that we experience. Common mental states include sensations, thoughts, beliefs, desires and volitions. As philosopher J.P Moreland explains in the following quote, these states are quite different from physical states. The initial section is actually in

Moreland's end notes, but I thought it would be worthwhile to see that first to establish definitions. This is extremely rich and mind-blowing material, and worth reading several times to digest it, if necessary:

This argument will assume a commonsense understanding of sensations, thoughts, beliefs, desires and volitions. For those unclear on these terms:

- A sensation is a state of awareness or sentience, a mode of consciousness for example, a conscious awareness of sound, color, or pain. Some sensations are experiences of things outside me like a tree or table. Others are awarenesses of other states within me like pains or itches. Emotions are types of sensations.

- A thought is a mental content that can be expressed in an entire sentence. A thought is the mental content of a statement. Some thoughts logically entail other thoughts. For example "All dogs are mammals"

entails "This dog is a mammal." If the former is true, the latter must be true. Some thoughts don't entail other thoughts, but merely provide evidence for them. For example, certain thoughts about evidence in a court case provide evidence for the thought that a person is guilty "He said he would kill him" provides evidence for the thought "He is the murderer."

- A belief is a person's view, accepted to varying degrees of strength, of how things really are. If a person has a belief (e.g., someone believes that it is raining), then that belief serves as the basis for the person's tendency or readiness to act as if the thing believed were really so (e.g., she gets an umbrella). At any given time, one can have many beliefs that are not currently being contemplated.

- A desire is a certain inclination to do, have, or experience certain things. Desires are either conscious or such that they can be made conscious through certain activities, for example, through therapy.

- An volition is a act of will or choice, an exercise of power, an endeavoring to do a certain thing, usually for the sake of some purpose or end. (2):

Mental states may be caused by physical states, and physical states may be caused by mental states. A feeling of pain (mental state) may be caused by being stuck with a pin (physical state), and one's arm going up (physical state) may be caused by an intention to vote (mental state). But just because A causes B, that does not mean that A is the same thing as B! Fire causes smoke, but fire is not smoke itself. Being stuck by a pin causes pain, but being stuck by a pin is not pain itself. A desire to vote causes one's arm to go up, but that desire is different than the arm's going up. The fact that a state of one's mind can affect physical states and the fact that physical states can affect the state of one's mind do not mean that corresponding mental and physical states are identical to each other. In fact, they are fundamentally different.

We know that mental states are in no sense physical (i.e. part of the physical, material world) because they possess four features not owned by physical states.

First, there is a raw qualitative feel--a "what it is like to have it"--to a mental state. For example, pain hurts. A physical state may cause pain, but the physical state itself can be completely described in the vocabulary of physics and chemistry, or in the commonsense vocabulary of the physical world. Being hurtful, however, is not describable in the vocabulary of any of these.

Second, many mental states have intentionality; "ofness" or "aboutness" which is directed towards an object. A thought, for instance, is about the moon. But no physical state is about anything. The brain is a physical object, but a brain state cannot be about the moon any more than a rock or a cloud can be about the moon. Only a state of mind can be about the moon.

Third, mental states are internal, private and immediately accessible to the subject having them. A scientist can know more about my brain than I do. But I have direct knowledge of my mind which is not available to anyone else.

Fourth, mental states fail to have crucial features that characterize physical states. Unlike physical states, they have no spatial extension (it doesn't make sense to ask how tall or wide someone's thoughts are) and they have no location either (which is why it doesn't make sense to ask where someone's thoughts are). In general, mental states cannot be described using physical language. (1)

Now if Darwinian evolution were *true*, it would have to adequately explain how it could produce every phenomenon of mental states through random mutations and natural selection. As Moreland points out in the following paragraphs, Darwinism has not come anywhere close to meeting this necessity. Moreland continues:

Given that mental states (states of mind) are immaterial and not physical, there are at least two reasons why evolutionary theory cannot explain their existence.

Something from nothing: According to evolutionary theory, before consciousness appeared, the universe contained nothing but matter and energy. The naturalistic story of the cosmos' evolution involves the rearrangement of the atomic parts of this matter into increasingly more complex structures according to natural law. Matter is brute mechanical, physical stuff. Consciousness, however, is immaterial and nonphysical. Physical reactions do not seem capable of generating consciousness. Some say the physical reactions that occur in the brain are capable of producing consciousness, yet brains seem too similar to other parts of the body (both brains and bodies are collections of cells totally describable in physical terms). How can like causes produce radically different effects? Though evolutionary theory can handle the appearance of the physical brain, the appearance of the nonphysical mind is utterly unpredictable and inexplicable. Thus the emergence of minds and consciousness seems to be a case of getting something from nothing.

The inadequacy of evolutionary explanations: Naturalists claim that evolutionary explanations can be offered for the appearance of all organisms and their parts. In principle, an evolutionary account could be given for increasingly complex physical structures that constitute different organisms. One of the driving forces behind Charles Darwin's exposition of evolution was the belief that all mental phenomena could be explained as features of physical objects. However, if minds and consciousness exist, they would be beyond the explanatory scope of evolutionary theory, and this would threaten the theory's plausibility.

Of course, theists think that minds and consciousness do, in fact, exist. But because naturalistic forms of evolution have proven incapable of explaining minds and consciousness, their existence has been rejected by naturalists.

I'll interject here to clarify what I think Moreland is saying. Many naturalists have "painted themselves into a corner" of rejecting the existence of free will, because if to admit our free will is to admit that something exists that can't be explained by solely physical processes (namely, Darwinism). Remember, Darwinism requires that all causal activity is due to physical processes ("event causation"). Free will necessarily depends on the other causational option: "agent causation".

Although we rarely have occasion to ponder this subject, I think a common sense assessment of it generally results in a chuckle, as this opinion is self-refuting. After all, why think you came to a sound conclusion if you don't actually have free will? The denial of free will may be the king of all self-refuting positions, but surprisingly, there are people with PhD's who believe in it.

Anyway, continuing with Moreland's piece, below he quotes atheist "naturalist" Paul Churchland prior to assessing his viewpoint:

The naturalist's question begging rejection of mind
(According to naturalist Paul Churchland):

The important point about the standard evolutionary story is that the human species and all of its features are the wholly physical outcome of a purely physical process. ... If this is the correct account of our origins, then there seems neither need, nor room, to fit any nonphysical substances or properties [such as minds and mental states] into our theoretical account of ourselves. We are creatures of matter. And we should learn to live with that fact.'(3)

Here, Churchland claims that, since we are merely the result of an entirely physical process (that of evolutionary theory), which works on wholly physical materials, we are wholly physical beings. But if, by saying "there seems neither need, nor room, to fit any nonphysical substances or properties into our theoretical account of ourselves," Churchland is saying that naturalistic evolutionary theory can adequately explain the nature of man, his argument clearly begs the question.4 This can be seen in the following outline of Churchland's argument:

(1) If we are merely the result of naturalistic, evolutionary processes, we are wholly physical beings.

(2) We are merely the result of naturalistic, evolutionary processes.

(3) Therefore, we are wholly physical beings.

Naturalists like Churchland accept premise (2). But why should we accept it? Those who think consciousness and mind are real do not. They argue:

(4) If we are merely the result of naturalistic, evolutionary processes, then we are wholly physical beings. (5) We possess nonphysical conscious minds, so we are not wholly physical beings.

(6) Therefore, we are not merely the result of naturalistic, evolutionary processes.

Naturalists argue for (3) on the basis of (2), but (5) and (6) show us that the truth of (2) assumes the truth of (3). Put another way, nobody will not think that (2) is true unless they already think that (3) is true — but (3) is exactly the point in question. The naturalist's argument assumes the very thing it's trying to prove.

As we saw above, the existence of minds and consciousness would threaten evolutionary theory's plausibility. The naturalistic explanation of the nature of man, however, begs the question by simply assuming that we are wholly physical beings. It gives us no reason to think that minds and consciousness do not exist.

The real issue, then, is the evidence for and against the immaterial, nonphysical nature of minds and consciousness. If the evidence is good, then we should embrace the idea that mental states and physical states are essentially different and that evolutionary theory cannot account for the former. But we have seen that the evidence is good. Mental states possess four features not owned by physical states, and evolutionary theory seems fundamentally incapable of explaining the existence of mental states. This means not only that the evolutionary argument fails but also that there will never be a complete naturalistic account of the nature and origin of human consciousness.

It will not do to claim that consciousness simply "emerged" from matter when it reached a certain level of complexity because "emergence" is merely a label for (rather than an explanation of) the phenomena being explained. Since we are made in God's image, there should be something about us that can't be adequately explained without postulating God's existence. And that is the case with mind and consciousness. Their reality supports the falsity of naturalism and the truth of theism." (2) [emphases mine, to distinguish Moreland's words from his paraphrasing of Churchland's thoughts.]

"Dualism" (the concept of body and soul as separate entities) is taught in the Bible. Many phenomena connected with near-death experiences seem to indicate that body and mind are separate entities. There are many documented incidents of people in near-death states who claimed to have "floated above their bodies", which support this concept of dualism. In many of these incidents, the subjects have reported information that they could not have gathered otherwise.

Examples include: reporting the number painted on top of an ambulance, describing a particular tennis shoe on the roof of a hospital, and reporting data from medical machinery that are facing away from the patient who had been wheeled into the hospital room nearly dead.

In other cases, the patients reported events that occurred in other rooms on different floors in the hospital. In one particularly amazing case, a little girl in a near-death state reported conversations that happened at that time between family members at her home over a mile away. There are dozens of documented cases with no plausible explanation aside from the essence (soul) of the person somehow leaving the body and returning with newly acquired information.

So we have both: 1) philosophical reflection on mental states, and 2) near-death experience phenomena that support the notion that human beings have souls, and are not solely physical entities. Some of the reasoning that can be engaged in by our minds/souls offers further support for a Creator, as we will see in the next chapter.

Meanwhile, here is an (incomplete) list of Nobel Prize-winning Scientists – including some very "heavy-hitters" in the recent history of Science -- who rejected a neo-Darwinist understanding of consciousness:

Wolfgang Pauli, Brian Josephson, William Phillips, Joseph Murray, Richard Smalley, Sir Nevill Mott, Christian Anfinsen, George Wald, Charles Townes, Eugene Wigner, Werner Heisenberg, Alexander Fleming, Erwin Schroedinger, Abdus Salam, Sir Charles Sherrington, Holly Compton, Sir John Eccles, Robert Millikan, Ernst Boris Chain, Niels Bohr, Guglielmo Marconi, Max Planck, Charles Richet, Sir William Crookes, Sir Joseph John Thompson, Lord Rayleigh (John William Strutt), Marie Curie, and Pierre Curie (http://www.uncommondescent.com/intelligent-design/twenty-one-more-famous-nobel-prize-winners-who-rejected-darwinism-as-an-account-of-consciousness/).

A NASA supercomputer; a creature without free will
(http://nonsense-verse.blogspot.com/2011/10/nasa-supercomputer-tackles-secrets-of.html).

CHAPTER SIX: THE AXIOLOGICAL (MORAL) ARGUMENT

"Stop everything
I think I hear the president
The pied piper of the tv screen
Is gonna make it simple
And he's got it all mapped out
And illustrated with cartoons
Too hard for clever folks to understand
They're more used to words like:
Ideology . . .
They're not talkin' 'bout right and left
They're talkin' 'bout

Right and wrong - do you know the difference
Right and wrong - do you know the difference
'tween the right and the left and the east and the
west
What you know and the things that you'll never
see."

~from *"Right and Wrong"*, by Joe Jackson

"Objective" (or "absolute") moral values are those values which truly exist regardless of whether anybody agrees with them or not. For example, if the Nazis had managed to exterminate or convert everyone who disagreed with them such that there was not a single living human being in opposition to their policies, objective morality would still hold that they were wrong, despite its having no living adherents.

If there were no objective moral values, then what the Nazis did would not be really wrong, even if 100% of the people thought that they were not wrong. Objective moral values are those which will be true even if every human being ceases to exist, or ceases to believe in them. Any less-grounded morality is known as "subjective", (or "relative") morality. For anything to be truly "evil" and not just subjectively objectionable, it must be a violation of objective morality.

We know intuitively that things like "don't steal" and "don't kill" are objectively good morals, but have you ever wondered if it's possible for objective morals like these to exist without God? Atheists often claim that God is not necessary for objective moral values and duties to exist, but to date there has never been a plausible alternative to God offered as an "anchor" for these values and duties.

The late J. L. Mackie of Oxford University, one of the most influential atheists of our time, admitted:

> If...there are...objective values, they make the existence of a god more probable than it would have been without them. Thus, we have a defensible argument from morality to the existence of God.(1)

Amazingly though, in order to maintain his atheism, Mackie then went on to deny that objective moral values exist. He also wrote:

> It is easy to explain this moral sense as a natural product of biological and social evolution. (2)

Friedrich Nietzsche, the atheist thinker of the 19th century who proclaimed the death of God, understood that the death of God meant the dissolution of all meaning and value in life. Nietzsche later went insane, which seems to be an indication that he was correct in his understanding of the implications of atheism. If we are nothing but a random accident in a treacherous, mindless universe, doomed to perish in a relatively short time (and, relatively speaking, not much before the eventual heat-death of the entire universe), what's the point? Any meaning, value and purpose we imagine under such conditions has no more significance than random atom collisions.

It's important to note that the question is not "Can we live moral lives without believing in God?", or "Can we recognize the existence of objective moral values without reference to God?". The relevant question is: "If God does not exist, do objective moral values exist?"

The formal **Axiological (Moral) Argument** for the existence of God goes as follows:

1) If God did not exist, objective moral values and duties would not exist.

2) Objective moral values and duties do exist.

3) Therefore, God exists.

Let's examine these propositions one at a time.

Regarding proposition #1), if God does not exist, we as human beings are simply chance arrangements of atoms, without any certainty that our mental faculties are unbiased, and without any transcendent grounding point for our morals. Furthermore, as atheist philosopher of science Michael Ruse puts it:

> *The position of the modern evolutionist...is that humans have an awareness of morality...because such an awareness is of biological worth. Morality is a biological adaptation no less than are hands and feet and teeth.... (3)*

Considered as a rationally justifiable set of claims about an objective something, ethics is illusory. I appreciate that when somebody says 'Love thy neighbor as thyself', they think they are referring above and beyond themselves...Nevertheless,...such reference is truly without foundation. Morality is just an aid to survival and reproduction,...and any deeper meaning is illusory. (4)

If there is no God who serves as an "anchor point" for morality, then it doesn't matter what anyone thinks is moral; any perceived morality is simply an opinion. "Majority Opinion" obviously cannot suffice as a source of objective morality, as there are numerous cases in history in which the majority was clearly wrong. A couple examples of that would be the Spanish Inquisition which killed several thousand in that particular culture, and Nazi Germany under Hitler which killed millions.

In addition, if there is no God, there is no transcendent entity to whom any duty is "owed", and without such an entity, there are no objective moral duties. Without moral duties, there can be no objective moral values. Actions like rape or "ethnic cleansing" meet the Darwinian objectives of survival and propagation of one's own "kind", so on a truly atheistic viewpoint they cannot be dismissed as immoral. Nevertheless, I think most of us recognize deep down that somehow these actions are reprehensible, whether or not we can articulate exactly why.

Now let's look at #2). When we witness or hear about horrendous things like a rape or a murder, we know deep down inside that it's not just unpleasant, but that it is wrong. Alternatively, when we consider things like love, honesty and self-sacrifice, it seems obvious to us that these things are more than simply preferable, but that they are actually good. This is the point where certain atheists will find themselves in a dilemma, as it follows that without God there can be no objective morals, but many find themselves unable to live with the implications of this belief.

Many atheists will claim on the one hand that there are no truly objective moral values, then on the other will condemn things like The Crusades and The Inquisition as moral abominations, and as objectively wrong!

A common sense reflection on this suggests that we all have a moral compass built into us, that is disturbed when we become aware of something that is truly wrong, and inspired when we witness something good. Many atheists claim that this is a result of Darwinian evolution, but they are not able to live with the implications of this worldview—a worldview which claims that objective moral values do not truly exist.

The following sentence is a simple demonstration of how wrong their worldview is: "If objective moral values do not exist, what Hitler did in Nazi Germany was not truly wrong". There are numerous other abominable human actions one could substitute into that statement as examples that would make the same case.

In conclusion then, if God did not exist, then no truly objective moral values would exist.

Since in addition to all of the other good reasons we have to believe in God, we know fully well in our hearts that objective moral values do exist, we have another indisputable piece of evidence that God is real.

There's no more reason to deny the objective reality of moral values than the objective reality of the physical world. Actions like rape, torture, and child abuse aren't just socially unacceptable behavior--they're moral abominations. Some things, at least, are really wrong. Similarly, love, equality, and self-sacrifice are really good. But if objective values cannot exist without God, and objective values do exist, then it follows logically and inescapably that God exists.

Adolf Hitler and Benito Mussolini, June 1940 (NARA)

CHAPTER SEVEN: THE ARGUMENT FROM THE RESURRECTION OF JESUS CHRIST

"In my time of dying, want nobody to mourn
All I want for you to do is take my body home

Well, well, well, so I can die easy

Well, well, well, so I can die easy

Jesus, gonna make up my dyin' bed.
Meet me, Jesus, meet me. Meet me in the middle
of the air
If my wings should fail me, Lord, please meet me
with another pair".

~from *"In my Time of Dying",* by Led Zeppelin

<u>Sherlock Holmes and the Secret Weapon (1943)</u> from
Public Domain Treasure Chest

Have you ever thought about what you would
really die for? That term has been thrown around
so much that it's easy to lose sight of its meaning,
but think about that question. For many, there is
nothing that they would actually willfully die for,
except perhaps accepting a quick death to avoid
an even more painful death. Ten of Jesus Christ's
disciples, plus Paul and His half-brother James,

were tortured and killed for believing in Him and not recanting their belief in Him. Given the fact that self-preservation is our most primal instinct, what does this tell us about what they saw?

In addition to accounts from within the Bible, there are numerous confirmations of early Christian martyrdom from secular history. Of all of these, the ones that should get our attention are the events in which purported eyewitnesses to the resurrection of Jesus Christ were put to death.

Think about it; if the resurrection of Christ did not happen, these individuals would know that fact, since they claimed to be eyewitnesses to it. Although people such as terrorists often die for things that are untrue, in those events, the individuals believed that particular lie to be true (such as the 9/11 terrorists believing that they will be rewarded for their actions). Throughout recorded history, there is no other record of people ever dying for something that they know is a lie—human instinct for self-preservation is too strong.

Now consider these facts:

The majority of New Testament scholars (Christian and non-Christian alike) agree that:

1) Christ was crucified and buried.

2) Somehow, despite a Roman Guard and a huge stone over it (that probably had a Roman seal on it), the tomb was found empty the following Sunday by a group of Christ's women followers, followed by several of His disciples.

3) With amazing suddenness, the previously flaky and frightened disciples claimed to have seen Him risen, followed by his half-brother James, and many others.

4) Not long afterwards, the apostle Paul made the same claim.

5) Subsequently, 10 of the 12 original disciples (all except for Judas and John), Jesus' half-brother James and the apostle Paul, experienced brutal floggings, beatings, imprisonment, and eventual martyrdom for not recanting their faith.

As death is our most primal fear, how then do we explain their willingness to go to their death? They saw something that made them unafraid of death and any other brutality. In the cases of Paul, James, and Jude, they were non-believers prior to their exposure to the resurrected Christ, and only thereafter became believers. They all knew the grimness of execution beforehand--it happened publicly with great frequency in those days. Take a look at how they died:

Andrew: Crucified.

Bartholomew: Crucified.

James, son of Alphaeus: Crucified.

James, son of Zebedee: Death by the sword.

Matthew: Death by the sword.

Peter: Crucified upside-down at his own request (he did not feel worthy to be crucified in the same manner as his Lord).

Philip: Crucified.

Simon the Zealot: Crucified.

Thaddaeus: Death by arrows.

Thomas: Death by a spear thrust.

James, son of Joseph: Death by the sword.

Paul: Beheaded

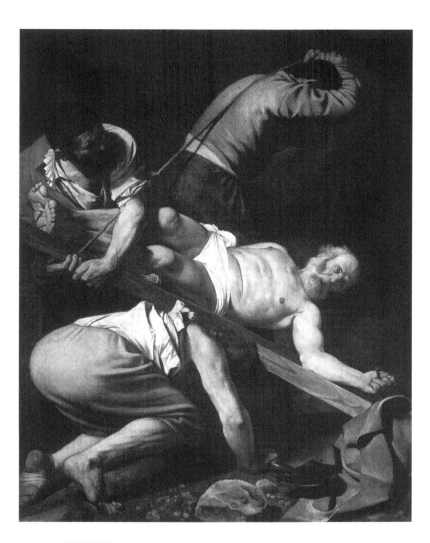

Crucifixion of St. Peter" by Caravaggio

If the resurrection didn't actually occur, these men would have known that, as they were eyewitnesses to it (1 Cor. 15:5-8). We can say with certainty then, that these men did not go to their deaths for a lie--they were willing to go to their deaths because they saw Jesus Christ resurrected, just as the Bible states that He was.

The historical facts of the life of Jesus of Nazareth make no sense if He was not resurrected. New Testament critics agree that He arrived on the scene about 2000 years ago with an unprecedented appearance and self-perception of divine authority; the authority and ability to stand and speak in God's place. This is why the Jewish Sanhedrin of the day instigated his brutal crucifixion for the charge of blasphemy. His claim was that in Himself the Kingdom of God had come, and he performed a sustained ministry of miracle-working and exorcisms as visible demonstrations of this fact. The supreme culmination of this claim, however, was his resurrection from the dead. If in fact Jesus was resurrected from the dead, then clearly we have evidence of a divine miracle on our hands and, therefore, evidence for the existence of God.

Now many people think that Jesus' resurrection is just something you believe in strictly by faith. As it turns out, however, there are three well-established facts, recognized by the majority of New Testament historians today, which support the case for the resurrection of Jesus: the discovery of empty tomb; Jesus' post-death appearances; and the sudden origin of the disciples' belief in His resurrection. Let's take a closer look at each of these (hat-tip to William Lane Craig for the basis of this formulation):

Historical Fact #1: On the Sunday following his crucifixion, Jesus' tomb was found empty by a group of his women followers. The location of the tomb was well-known to Jews, Greeks and Romans alike. There is no chance that they were looking at the wrong tomb. According to Jacob Kremer, an Austrian scholar who has specialized in the study of the resurrection, "By far most scholars hold firmly to the reliability of the Biblical statements about the empty tomb." (1) According to the New Testament critic, D.H. van Daalen, "it is extremely difficult to object to the empty tomb on historical grounds; those who deny it do so on the basis of theological or philosophical assumptions". (2)

Historical Fact #2: On multiple, separate occasions, and in various circumstances, different individuals and groups saw appearances of Jesus alive after his death. According to the prominent, skeptical German New Testament critic Gerd Ludemann, "It may be taken as historically certain that...the disciples had experiences after Jesus' death in which Jesus appeared to them as the risen Christ." (3) These appearances were witnessed not only by believers, but also by unbelievers, skeptics (such as Jesus' half-brother James), and even enemies (such as Saul of Tarsus, who later became the Apostle Paul).

Historical Fact #3: The original disciples (and many others) suddenly and sincerely came to believe in the resurrection of Jesus, despite having every predisposition to the contrary. The Jews had come to believe that their Messiah would be "Maschiach ben David" (Messiah Son of David), the Conquering King who would vanquish their

Roman oppressors and set up the Millenial Kingdom. They believed this based on Old Testament prophecies of the Second Coming of Christ. They had largely forgotten about prophecies like Isaiah 52-53 and Psalm 22, which spoke of the First Coming of Christ. Therefore they really had no belief in a dying, much less a rising, Messiah, and Jewish beliefs about the afterlife precluded anyone's rising from the dead prior to the end of the world. According to Luke Johnson, a New Testament scholar at Emory University, "Some sort of powerful, transformative experience is required to generate the sort of movement earliest Christianity was..." (4) N. T. Wright, an eminent British scholar, concludes, "That is why, as an historian, I cannot explain the rise of early Christianity unless Jesus rose again, leaving an empty tomb behind him." (5)

So, after the crucifixion you have 11 disciples devastated in fear and dismay, along with Jesus' non-believing brothers (James and Jude), and homicidal enemy (Paul), all with no reason to believe, and every reason not to. Then suddenly, along with hundreds more (1

Corinthians 15, Acts 2), they suddenly and simultaneously become zealous witnesses to His resurrection, maintaining this belief steadfastly all the way through years of hideous persecutions and death.

Perhaps the most popular naturalistic theory that has been adopted in order to account for these facts is the hallucination hypothesis, which holds that these appearances were simply simultaneous visions of the risen Christ. But just think about this for a minute; do you think it's plausible that hundreds of people suddenly and spontaneously had the exact same detailed hallucinations over the course of 40 days? In all the annals of psychology, there has never been documentation of corporate hallucinations (that is, the same, detailed hallucinations being experienced by different people). Moreover, these appearances occurred to individuals, and various different-sized groups, at different places, and at different times over the course of 40 days.

Perhaps the second most-often endorsed non-resurrection theory is the "swoon" hypothesis, which holds that Jesus didn't actually die, but rather went unconscious. On this view, He "came to" after being sealed in the tomb and somehow found a way to move the two-ton boulder that was affixed to the entrance, then snuck past the Roman guards that were posted there without their noticing. As any good doctor will tell you, this theory is beyond ridiculous, as there is no chance anyone would have survived indescribably brutal Roman floggings (some would die from this alone), beatings, hours nailed to a cross, and a spear thrust into his side. Roman soldiers were brutally efficient killers, and suffered the ultimate punishment (their own execution) if they mistakenly allowed someone to live who had been condemned to death.

If one were to boil the above into a propositional argument and infer what it entails about Theism, it might go like this:

The Resurrection of Jesus Argument

1. There are three established facts concerning the fate of Jesus of Nazareth: the discovery of his empty tomb, his post-mortem appearances, and the origin of his disciples' belief in his resurrection.

2. The hypothesis "God raised Jesus from the dead" is the best explanation of these facts.

3. The hypothesis "God raised Jesus from the dead" entails that the God revealed by Jesus of Nazareth exists.

4. Therefore, the God revealed by Jesus of Nazareth exists.

We've already seen ample evidence from the creation of the universe and several other phenomena that the supernatural is possible. In the next chapter we will examine some prophecies that were recorded in the Old Testament that came to pass years later. These fulfilled prophecies bury the mathematical possibility of chance fulfillment under mounds of irrefutable evidence. Remember, any occurrence with smaller odds than 1 in 10 to the 50th power is not possible by chance alone. If Jesus Christ fulfilled the Messianic prophecies against all odds, is there really any plausible alternative explanation other than that He is the Son of God, sent to be crucified on our behalf, and to rise again confirming that He was indeed the prophesied Messiah? Consider that question as we look at fulfilled prophecy in the next chapter.

CHAPTER EIGHT: THE HISTORICAL VERACITY OF SCRIPTURE

"Thy word is a lamp unto my feet
And a light unto my path.
Thy word is a lamp unto my feet
And a light unto my path.

When I feel afraid,
And think I've lost my way.
Still, youre there right beside me.
Nothing will I fear
As long as you are near;
Please be near me to the end.

Thy word is a lamp unto my feet
And a light unto my path.
Thy word is a lamp unto my feet
And a light unto my path."

~from *"Thy Word"*, Traditional

Archaeological dig of Second Temple era structures.
Credit: Reuters/Ammar Awad

If you, like many people, have rejected the Bible from consideration due to scriptures that don't seem plausible or God-inspired, I urge you to be careful about this. I had done so myself when I was young -- partially due to lame explanations that had been given to me, partially due to sketchy translations, and also due to my own aversion to anything resembling "rules". Regarding the latter, as I learned to play music, I eventually realized that certain rules (like improvising within a particular musical scale) can create freedoms that allow you to soar to heights unimaginable without them. Regarding the former two points, I ask you to recognize a pair of simple principles, and reserve judgment until you've finished this book:

1) Ancient Hebrew had about 1000 times less words in it than modern English does. This means that each Hebrew word had on average far, far more possible meanings than our English does. There are tons of bad translations (and bad translators) floating around out there. Try to look at different translations of the verses that concern you to see if there is a different rendering of it that makes more sense to you. There are also great sites on the Internet (like www.Blueletterbible.org) that have a built in concordance where you can look up each word in any passage and check the definition of the original Greek, Hebrew or Aramaic word to see if it's being handled objectively, and also switch translations with the click of a button. I am continually finding resolutions to scripture

challenges after 30 years of Bible study, so believe me, it's worth a long look.

2) If you find that no translation of particular passages is plausible to you, and you are certain that you have thought it through completely (be honest now!), recognize that the only thing at stake is the concept of "inerrancy". If one were to grant this possibility, "the core" of the Bible could still simultaneously be true! Theoretically at least, the possibility exists that God inspired the original, but that man (the scribe and/or translator) messed it up somewhere along the line, maybe in numerous cases. If this is so, there is no reason to throw out "the baby" (the "core", which has about 2000 fulfilled prophecies testifying to it, and over 25,000 archaeological discoveries confirming it) with the bathwater (whatever segments might possibly have been imperfectly recorded or translated). In fact, it would be downright illogical to do so, as the notion that these prophecies were fulfilled by chance is not mathematically plausible. Whatever conclusion one derives, it has to account for these

prophecy fulfillments, and thus, I think it necessarily involves the supernatural.

Imagine you're in a court of law and the prosecution is cross-examining the defense witness and the defense witness submits a document that testifies about the person and events in question. Let's say the document consists of 66 smaller documents, written by 40 different persons, from different walks of life, in different parts of the world, during different times, spanning 1,600 years, and were in 3 different languages. Moreover, they together had about 2000 specific and detailed predictive prophecies about events that seemed extremely unlikely, which were clearly fulfilled at a later date in time. Within these roughly 2000 prophecies, 61 are very specific prophecies about one particular man who was to later walk the earth, carry out a ministry of miracles and exorcisms, be persecuted and executed in very specific ways. The teachings of this one individual, by the way, would harmonize the remainder of this document into an explanatory whole, in a way that would make sense of our existence in this time-space continuum. What would be the odds that such a document would be consistent and predictively flawless by random chance? The odds would be effectively zero.

What would the prosecution do to disprove this document? All the prosecution would have to do is show one predictive prophecy unfulfilled in its time, since that would indicate an error. What would be the prosecution's first step? The first step would be to read the Bible from cover to cover. You cannot prove or disprove the statements in a book until you've first read them. Remarkably, many of the loudest critics of the Bible have not actually studied the book, but rather have relied on excerpts and hearsay to attack it. If they were to actually do so, they'd be in for a surprise.

Cave at Qumran where some of the Dead Sea Scrolls were found

Let's look at just some of the prophecies pointing to the man called Jesus Christ. The following calculations were made by Dr. Peter Stoner (former Chairman of the Departments of Mathematics and Astronomy at Pasadena City College) along with a team of graduate students, and were published in his book Science Speaks. They show that coincidence is ruled out by the science of probability.

Stoner and his team determined that by applying this modern science to eight prophecies

(Micah 5:2, Mal. 3:1, Zech. 9:9, Zech. 13:6, Zech. 11:12, Zech. 11:13, Isa. 53:7, and Ps. 22:16), "we find that the chance that any man might have lived down to the present time and fulfilled all eight prophecies is 1 in 10^{17}." (1) That would be 1 in 100,000,000,000,000,000!

In order to help us comprehend this staggering probability, Stoner illustrates it by supposing that "we take 10^{17} silver dollars and lay them on the face of Texas. They will cover all of the state two feet deep. Now mark one of these silver dollars and stir the whole mass thoroughly, all over the state. Blindfold a man and tell him that he can travel as far as he wishes, but he must pick up one silver dollar and say that this is the right one. What chance would he have of getting the right one? Just the same chance that the prophets would have had of writing these eight prophecies and having them all come true in any one man."

To take it further, the odds of Jesus fulfilling just 48 of the major prophecies concerning Him are 1 in 10^{157}; that is a one with 157 zeros behind it. By comparison, the estimated number of atoms in the entire known universe is about 10^{80} (that is a one with 80 zeros to the right of it). In considering 48 prophecies, Stoner says, "we find the chance that any one man fulfilled all 48 prophecies to be 1 in 10^{157}" (2), or 1 in 1,000,000,000,000,000,000,000,000,000,000, 000,000,000,000,000,000,000,000,000,000,000,00 0,000,000,000,000,000,000,000,000,000,000,000, 000,000,000,000,000,000,000,000,000,000,000,00 0,000,000,000,000,000,000,000.

The estimated number of atoms in the universe is around 10^{80}, so the odds of selecting one particular atom in the entire universe on your first try is far, far greater than for Jesus to have accidentally fulfilled these prophecies. It should be quite evident by now that Jesus did not fulfill these prophecies by accident. This could not have happened by even deliberate manipulation. There must have been some kind of supernatural assistance involved.

Regarding Peter Stoner's book Science Speaks that initially published these odds, the American Scientific Affiliation endorsed its scientific content and prophecy probability calculations. Even if one disagrees with some of the details in these calculations, the fact that these events are against tremendous odds is inescapable.

You can demonstrate the truth of the bible by cross-examining it like a witness on a witness stand in a court of law. If you do so you will find that it is a trustworthy witness. The Bible testifies about Jesus Christ (John 5:39) and is "written that you may believe that Jesus is the Christ, the Son of God, and that by believing you may have life in his name." John 20:31 (NIV) and so "you may know that you have eternal life." (NIV) 1 John 5:13 .

Given the importance of this document it is no wonder God gave us so much evidence. One does not have to believe in Jesus Christ on "faith alone"; He has not left us without evidence. In the words of Jesus Christ:

"This is the verdict; Light has come into the world, but men loved darkness instead of light because their deeds were evil." John 3:19 (NIV).

When you've finished this book, ask yourself "What will the verdict be with me?"

Let's look at some more in-depth analyses of a few Biblical prophecies published by former Cal Tech scientist Hugh Ross, Ph.D:

Fulfilled Prophecy: Evidence for the Reliability of the Bible

Unique among all books ever written, the Bible accurately foretells specific events-in detail-many years, sometimes centuries, before they occur. Approximately 2500 prophecies appear in the pages of the Bible, about 2000 of which already have been fulfilled to the letter—no errors. (The remaining 500 or so reach into the future and may be seen unfolding as days go by.) Since the probability for any one of these prophecies having been fulfilled by chance averages less than one in ten (figured very conservatively) and since the prophecies are for the most part independent of one another, the odds for all these prophecies *having been fulfilled by chance without error is less than one in 10^{2000} (that is 1 with 2000 zeros written after it)!*

God is not the only one, however, who uses forecasts of future events to get people's attention. Satan does, too. Through clairvoyants (such as Jeanne Dixon and Edgar Cayce), mediums, spiritists, and others, come remarkable predictions, though rarely with more than about 60 percent accuracy, never with total accuracy. Messages from Satan, furthermore, fail to match the detail of Bible prophecies, nor do they include a call to repentance.

The acid test for identifying a prophet of God is recorded by Moses in Deuteronomy 18:21-22. According to this Bible passage (and others), God's prophets, as distinct from Satan's spokesmen, are 100 percent accurate in their predictions. There is no room for error.

As economy does not permit an explanation of all the Biblical prophecies that have been fulfilled, what follows in a discussion of a few that exemplify the high degree of specificity, the range of projection, and/or the "supernature" of the predicted events. Readers are encouraged to select others, as well, and to carefully examine their historicity.

(1) Some time before 500 B.C. the prophet Daniel proclaimed that Israel's long-awaited Messiah would begin his public ministry 483 years after the issuing of a decree to restore and rebuild Jerusalem (Daniel 9:25-26). He further predicted that the Messiah would be "cut off," killed, and that this event would take place prior to a second destruction of Jerusalem. Abundant documentation shows that these prophecies were perfectly fulfilled in the life (and crucifixion) of Jesus Christ. The decree regarding the restoration of Jerusalem was issued by Persia's King Artaxerxes to the Hebrew priest Ezra in 458 B.C., 483 years later the ministry of Jesus Christ began in Galilee. (Remember that due to calendar changes, the date for the start of Christ's ministry is set by most historians at about 26 A.D. Also note that from 1 B.C. to 1 A.D. is just one year.) Jesus' crucifixion occurred only a few years later, and

about four decades later, in 70 A.D. came the destruction of Jerusalem by Titus.

(Probability of chance fulfillment = 1 in 10^5.)*

(2) In approximately 700 B.C. the prophet Micah named the tiny village of Bethlehem as the birthplace of Israel's Messiah (Micah 5:2). The fulfillment of this prophecy in the birth of Christ is one of the most widely known and widely celebrated facts in history.

(Probability of chance fulfillment = 1 in 10^5.)

(3) In the fifth century B.C. a prophet named Zechariah declared that the Messiah would be betrayed for the price of a slave—thirty pieces of silver, according to Jewish law-and also that this money would be used to buy a burial ground for Jerusalem's poor foreigners (Zechariah 11:12-13). Bible writers and secular historians both record thirty pieces of silver as the sum paid to Judas Iscariot for betraying Jesus, and they indicate that the money went to purchase a "potter's field," used—just as predicted—for the burial of poor aliens (Matthew 27:3-10).

(Probability of chance fulfillment = 1 in 10^{11}.)

(4) Some 400 years before crucifixion was invented, both Israel's King David and the prophet Zechariah described the Messiah's death in words that perfectly depict that mode of execution. Further, they said that the body would be pierced and that none of the bones would be broken, contrary to customary procedure in cases of crucifixion (Psalm 22 and 34:20; Zechariah 12:10). Again, historians and New Testament writers confirm the fulfillment: Jesus of Nazareth died on a Roman cross, and his extraordinarily quick death eliminated the need for the usual breaking of bones. A spear was thrust into his side to verify that he was, indeed, dead.

(Probability of chance fulfillment = 1 in 10^{13}.)

(5) The prophet Isaiah foretold that a conqueror named Cyrus would destroy seemingly impregnable Babylon and subdue Egypt along with most of the rest of the known world. This same man, said Isaiah, would decide to let the

Jewish exiles in his territory go free without any payment of ransom (Isaiah 44:28; 45:1; and 45:13). Isaiah made this prophecy 150 years before Cyrus was born, 180 years before Cyrus performed any of these feats (and he did, eventually, perform them all), and 80 years before the Jews were taken into exile.

(Probability of chance fulfillment = 1 in 10^{15}.)

(6) Mighty Babylon, 196 miles square, was enclosed not only by a moat, but also by a double wall 330 feet high, each part 90 feet thick. It was said by unanimous popular opinion to be indestructible, yet two Bible prophets declared its doom. These prophets further claimed that the ruins would be avoided by travelers, that the city would never again be inhabited, and that its stones would not even be moved for use as building material (Isaiah 13:17-22 and Jeremiah 51:26, 43). Their description is, in fact, the well-documented history of the famous citadel.

(Probability of chance fulfillment = 1 in 10^9.)

(7) The exact location and construction sequence of Jerusalem's nine suburbs was predicted by Jeremiah about 2600 years ago. He referred to the time of this building project as "the last days," that is, the time period of Israel's second rebirth as a nation in the land of Palestine (Jeremiah 31:38-40). This rebirth became history in 1948, and the construction of the nine suburbs has gone forward precisely in the locations and in the sequence predicted.

(Probability of chance fulfillment = 1 in 10^{18}.)

(8) The prophet Moses foretold (with some additions by Jeremiah and Jesus) that the ancient Jewish nation would be conquered twice and that the people would be carried off as slaves each time, first by the Babylonians (for a period of 70 years), and then by a fourth world kingdom (which we know as Rome). The second conqueror, Moses said, would take the Jews captive to Egypt in ships, selling them or giving them away as slaves to all parts of the world. Both of these predictions were fulfilled to the letter, the first in 607 B.C. and the second in 70 A.D. God's spokesmen said, further,

that the Jews would remain scattered throughout the entire world for many generations, but without becoming assimilated by the peoples or of other nations, and that the Jews would one day return to the land of Palestine to re-establish for a second time their nation (Deuteronomy 29; Isaiah 11:11-13; Jeremiah 25:11; Hosea 3:4-5 and Luke 21:23-24).

This prophetic statement sweeps across 3500 years of history to its complete fulfillment—in our lifetime.

(Probability of chance fulfillment = 1 in 10^{20}.)

(9) Jeremiah predicted that despite its fertility and despite the accessibility of its water supply, the land of Edom (today a part of Jordan) would become a barren, uninhabited wasteland (Jeremiah 49:15-20; Ezekiel 25:12-14). His description accurately tells the history of that now bleak region.

(Probability of chance fulfillment = 1 in 10^5.)

(10) Joshua prophesied that Jericho would be rebuilt by one man. He also said that the man's eldest son would die when the reconstruction began and that his youngest son would die when the work reached completion (Joshua 6:26). About five centuries later this prophecy found its fulfillment in the life and family of a man named Hiel (I Kings 16:33-34).

(Probability of chance fulfillment = 1 in 10^7).

(11) The day of Elijah's supernatural departure from Earth was predicted unanimously—and accurately, according to the eye-witness account—by a group of fifty prophets (II Kings 2:3-11).

(Probability of chance fulfillment = 1 in 10^9).

(12) Jahaziel prophesied that King Jehoshaphat and a tiny band of men would defeat an enormous, well-equipped, well-trained army without even having to fight. Just as predicted, the King and his troops stood looking on as their foes were supernaturally destroyed to the last man (II Chronicles 20).

(Probability of chance fulfillment = 1 in 10^8).

(13) One prophet of God (unnamed, but probably Shemiah) said that a future king of Judah, named Josiah, would take the bones of all the occultic priests (priests of the "high places") of Israel's King Jeroboam and burn them on Jeroboam's altar (I Kings 13:2 and II Kings 23:15-18). This event occurred approximately 300 years after it was foretold.

(Probability of chance fulfillment = 1 in 10^{13}).

Since these thirteen prophecies cover mostly separate and independent events, the probability of chance occurrence for all thirteen is about 1 in 10^{138} (138 equals the sum of all the exponents of 10 in the probability estimates above). For the sake of putting the figure into perspective, this probability can be compared to the statistical chance that the second law of thermodynamics will be reversed in a given situation (for example, that a gasoline engine will refrigerate itself during its combustion cycle or that heat will flow from a cold body to a hot body)

— that chance = 1 in 10^{80}. Stating it simply, based on these thirteen prophecies alone, the Bible record may be said to be vastly more reliable than the second law of thermodynamics. Each reader should feel free to make his own reasonable estimates of probability for the chance fulfillment of the prophecies cited here. In any case, the probabilities deduced still will be absurdly remote.

Given that the Bible proves so reliable a document, there is every reason to expect that the remaining 500 prophecies, those slated for the "time of the end," also will be fulfilled to the last letter. Who can afford to ignore these coming events, much less miss out on the immeasurable blessings offered to anyone and everyone who submits to the control of the Bible's author, Jesus Christ? Would a reasonable person take lightly God's warning of judgment for those who reject what they know to be true about Jesus Christ and the Bible, or who reject Jesus' claim on their lives?

*The estimates of probability included herein come from a group of secular research scientists. As an example of their method of *estimation, consider their calculations for this first prophecy cited:*

Since the Messiah's ministry could conceivably begin in any one of about 5000 years, there is, then, one chance in about 5000 that his ministry could begin in 26 A.D.

Since the Messiah is God in human form, the possibility of his being killed is considerably low, say less than one chance in 10.

Relative to the second destruction of Jerusalem, this execution has roughly an even chance of occurring before or after that event, that is, one chance in 2.

Hence, the probability of chance fulfillment for this prophecy is 1 in 5000 x 10 x 2, which is 1 in 100,000, or 1 in 10^5. (3)

Although there have been more than 25,000 archaeological discoveries that support the events in the Bible, there has never been a single discovery that conflicted with it. As a wise man once said, "The Bible is a book that nobody could invent if they would, and which nobody would invent if they could." God somehow supernaturally used the individual authors, all of whom "wrote as they were carried along by the Holy Spirit" to write what He intended, all the while maintaining their personal styles within each book in a way that stands out very uniquely among all of the world's literature as truly "one-of-a-kind".

I'm not aware of any comprehensive calculation that's been done on the above, but if we were to boil just the minimum improbability of prophecies fulfilled by Jesus (as calculated by Dr. Peter Stoner and his team) down into a propositional argument, it might go like this:

The Predictive Prophecy Fulfillment Argument

1. There are about 2000 predictive prophecies in the Bible that have been fulfilled, many of which are messianic, and refer to the first coming of Jesus Christ.

2. The odds against just 48 of these being fulfilled by chance alone is about 1 in 10^{158}.

3. According to probability theorists, anything with lower odds than 1 in 10^{50} is mathematically impossible.

4. Therefore, Christ's fulfillment of these prophecies is supernatural, and the other prophetic fulfillments add support to this conclusion.

CHAPTER NINE: THE SHROUD OF TURIN

"To pass beyond is what I seek, I fear that I may be too weak
And those are few who've seen it through to glimpse the other side,
The promised land is waiting like a maiden that is soon to be a bride
The moment is a masterpiece, the weight of indecision's in the air
It's standing there, the symbol and the sum of all that's me
It's just a travesty, towering, blocking out the light and blinding me
I want to see"

--from "The Wall" by Kansas

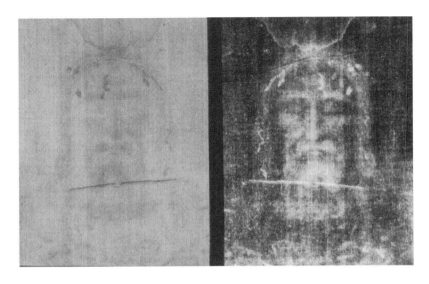

Positive and negative images of The Shroud side by side
(http://www.sacred-destinations.com/italy/turin-shroud)

The Shroud of Turin is a cloth approximately 14 feet long by 3 ½ feet wide, and bears a "photographically negative" image of a man who seemed to have suffered the exact violence that was done to Jesus Christ at His crucifixion. The Catholic Church zealously guards the Shroud, and has not allowed a great deal of direct analysis of it. The most intense scientific investigation of the Shroud was undertaken by the Shroud of Turin Research Project (STURP) in 1978, when a team of forensic scientists were granted the rare opportunity to examine the Shroud in detail over several days. These investigators determined that the Shroud is unlike any artifact the world has ever seen.

The image is "pixilated", meaning that it's made up of thousands of tiny dots. Each dot only penetrates partway into the topmost fibrils of the outer threads, each of which is about 1/10 the width of a human hair. According to the STURP report, "No pigments, paints, dyes or stains have been found on the fibrils. X-ray, fluorescence and microchemistry on the fibrils preclude the possibility of paint being used as a method for creating the image." (1) The dots appear to be the result of "oxidation, dehydration and conjugation", which suggests that they were produced by radiation. (2)

In 1988, a sample from the Shroud was carbon-dated to between 1260 and 1390 AD. To many, this was enough to write off the Shroud as a forgery, but new information that has arisen since those tests has cast substantial doubt on their veracity. One fact that has raised questions is a type of "bioplastic coating" (a kind of living varnish made of microorganisms) that can radically alter carbon-dating results. A bioplastic coating of this type was found on the Shroud by C-14 expert Dr. Leoncio Garza-Valdes.

Additionally, according to a report by a pair of scientists (*Benford and Merino*) in 2005, the section of cloth that was subjected to Carbon 14 dating included a 16th century dyed cotton repair that was not part of the original cloth (which is linen), but was expertly spliced and woven in by medieval nuns who were highly skilled at this type of repair.

One of the original STURP team members (and reportedly the most skeptical of all the Shroud researchers) was Los Alamos National Laboratory Chemist Dr. Ray Rogers. Rogers wrote Benford and Merino off as crackpots, and told fellow STURP team member Barrie Schwortz that he could disprove them in five minutes, because he had Shroud scraps left over from previous analysis. To Rogers' disbelief, however, he confirmed Benford and Merino's analysis. Further examination of X-ray Fluoroscopic photographs of

The Shroud further confirmed the existence of this contamination. The variance in the three dates from 1988 appears to match the apportionate extent to which they were "contaminated" by the cotton repairs. In light of this discovery, the 1988 dating could have been correct (or close), and yet it is invalid because it was examining impure samples.

In a book called *Il Mistero Della Sindone (The Mystery of the Shroud)* released in 2013 by an Italian scientist and professor named Giulio Fanti, more evidence for The Shroud's authenticity was presented. Dr. Fanti apparently got ahold of threads from The Shroud, and dated them to the time of Christ.

Hopefully, the Catholic Church will allow it to be tested again with better techniques, but especially in light of the discoveries of the cotton contamination and the bioplastic coating, the dating should be at least categorized as inconclusive until such time as new tests can be performed.

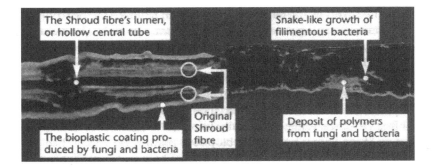

Microphotograph of microtomed shroud fibril by Dr. Garza-Valdez showing typical deposition of bioplastic coating and other fungal and bacterial accretion. From "The Blood and the Shroud" by Ian Wilson, 1998, The Free Press, NY, p225.

There are dozens of pieces of art and coins from the first millennium after Christ that appear to be copied from the Shroud image. Renowned Swiss criminologist Max Frei determined that particular types of limestone dust and pollen grains removed from the Shroud could only have come from in or around Jerusalem.

There is another artifact called "The Sudarium of Oviedo" located in Spain, which appears to be the head cloth of Jesus referenced in the gospels, and which is provenanced (traced via historical references) back to at least the 7th century AD. This artifact has bloodstains, also of type AB, which match those of the Shroud precisely when they are overlaid with one another.

When viewed with a complex device known as the VP-8 Image Analyzer, the image on the Shroud appears topographically 3-dimensional, strongly suggesting that the image was projected by a body while the cloth was draped over it. There is no known forgery that has this feature, which would be amazing for a forger to even imagine, much less engineer.

In addition, the blood stains have been positively identified as human blood exudates (type AB), and the flow patterns exactly match what would be expected in a crucifixion. There are pierce wounds in both feet and wrists, a large puncture wound to the torso, puncture wounds around the head, approximately 120 dumbbell-shaped contusions (matching the Roman "flagrum", which was a type of whip) and many other injuries.

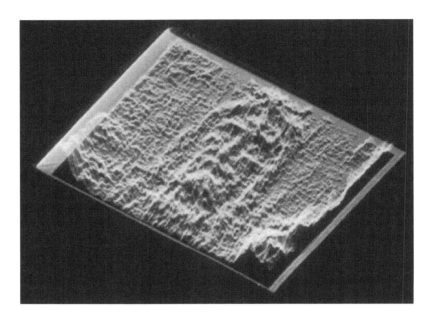

The Shroud in a VP-8 Image Analyzer - Image credit: Barrie Schwortz, Shroud.com

Much has been made of certain skeptical speculations on the Shroud made by a gentleman named Walter McCrone in the late 1970's. McCrone claimed that he had found paint particles on the Shroud, and that the image was therefore a painting. Many skeptics followed suit with similar claims, but the fact is that close analysis of the threads show that there is no correlation between the image and any paint particles. Moreover, there are 52 historically documented cases of artists "sanctifying" their paintings over the years by placing them face-to-face with the Shroud, which could plausibly explain the existence of paint particles on it.

As I noted previously, the image "pixels" only penetrate partway into the topmost fibrils of various threads, each of which is about 1/10th the width of a human hair. If the image was induced by anything liquid, there would be evidence of "wicking" (the soaking of the liquid into underlying material), but in this case there is none; the subtlety of whatever mechanism instigated the image is mind-boggling. The closest similarity to this type of image is the radiation "shadows' created by the atomic bomb blasts in Hiroshima and Nagasaki. In order to reproduce an image with this level of subtlety and precision, it would require a computer-driven atomic laser, a technology that does not yet exist.

Is the Shroud a subtle image left by the energy produced when Jesus Christ's body was resurrected? As of this writing, every other suggested hypothesis for its formation has been ruled out.

If we were to formulate a propositional argument based on the above, it might go something like this:

The Shroud of Turin Argument

1. Imaging experts say that to create the 3D image on the Shroud, one would need an atomic laser controlled by a supercomputer.

2. Such a device was not available to an ancient forger.

3. Therefore, a radiation imprint from the resurrection is a better explanation.

CHAPTER TEN: THE GRAND DESIGN TO DISMISS PHILOSOPHY (WITHOUT FREE WILL!)

"You can choose a ready guide in some celestial voice.
If you choose not to decide, you still have made a choice.
You can choose from phantom fears and kindness that can kill;
I will choose a path that's clear-
I will choose Free Will."

~from *"Freewill"* by Rush

Stephen Hawking may be the most well-known mathematician of all time. He recently retired from the Lucasian Professorship at Cambridge University, which was a chair once occupied by Sir Isaac Newton, and which he held since 1979. He has endured through several decades with the debilitating disease ALS (also known as "Lou Gehrig's Disease") which has earned him the respect of many, both in and out of the scholarly community.

While I respect Hawking's determination (and I honestly wish him the best, both here and hereafter), his assertions need to be weighed with the same careful scrutiny as those of others in the public sphere. In fact, I think it's axiomatic that anyone who opines on ultimate metaphysical questions is bound to have their assertions analyzed to a degree that roughly correlates with their level of influence in the world. Since many people (including some who are very close to me) have deferred to Hawking as if his opinions are unquestionable, and I wholeheartedly disagree with that proposition, I will be challenging them in this book.

Any doubt that Hawking has opened the door to this should be allayed by a self-refuting philosophical statement from the second paragraph in his latest book (co-authored with CalTech physicist Leonard Mlodonow) The Grand Design: "Philosophy is dead"(1). Unfortunately, it seems that Hawking's formidable acumen for mathematics is not matched by a concomitant understanding of logic, as neither he nor his co-author seems to realize that this is a philosophical statement. Let's look at the definition of the word "philosophy" from the American Heritage Dictionary:

1. Love and pursuit of wisdom by intellectual means and moral self-discipline.

2. Investigation of the nature, causes, or principles of reality, knowledge, or values, based on logical reasoning rather than empirical methods.[*Note: I bolded this sub-definition for emphasis, as it may be the one most relevantly ignored by Hawking/Mlodonow].

3. A system of thought based on or involving such inquiry: the philosophy of Hume.

4. The critical analysis of fundamental assumptions or beliefs.

5. The disciplines presented in university curriculums of science and the liberal arts, except medicine, law, and theology.

6. The discipline comprising logic, ethics, aesthetics, metaphysics, and epistemology.

7. A set of ideas or beliefs relating to a particular field or activity; an underlying theory: an original philosophy of advertising.

8. A system of values by which one lives: has an unusual philosophy of life.

Philosophy is dead?! That's a pretty bold claim, and an insult to many of Hawking's erstwhile colleagues at Cambridge, as well as professional academic philosophers worldwide. As a philosopher myself, I not only resent this remark, but I also resent the fact that this book seems: A) to have been slapped together from half-baked and self-referentially incoherent ideas, B) to be sprinkled throughout with snotty remarks about religion, and C) to be confusing people and causing them to think and say silly things.

Photo by Universal Studios Hollywood via Getty Images

Hawking and Mlodinow primarily attempt to answer three questions in this book:

     1. Why is there something rather than nothing?

     2. Why do we exist?

     3. Why this particular set of laws and not some other?

Strangely enough, # 2 gets "sucked into the vortex" of #1 and doesn't really receive a separate answer. They give two mutually-contradictory "answers" to # 1, both of which are absurd on their face (more on those below). The answer to # 3 acknowledges that there is incredible fine-tuning in the universe (as we saw in chapter two), but appeals to a speculative unscientific explanation -- a "multiverse" – as the explanation. The problem is that a multiverse, even if granted for the sake of discussion, itself begs the question of causation.

Hawking's contemporaries are not impressed with his latest offering. South African Cosmologist George Ellis (who worked with Hawking and Roger Penrose developing their singularity theorems) has been a Christian for a number of years, and finds Hawking's position to be incoherent. Ellis, the current President of the International Society for Science and Religion argued in response to The Grand Design:

"Philosophy is not dead. Every point of view is imbued with philosophy. Why is science worth doing? The answer is philosophical... Science can't answer that question about itself."(2)

Another giant English mind, that of Professor Chris Isham (a philosopher and theoretical physicist at Imperial College London, who was described by Paul Davies as "Britain's greatest quantum gravity expert") was similarly unimpressed. "I groaned when I read this" Isham stated. "Stephen's always saying this sort of thing... but I suspect he's never read a philosophy book in his life."(3)

Although much of the book is an incoherent mess, I've overheard it being discussed on a popular level as if it is significant. It seems to me that it's therefore worthwhile to understand some of its propositions in their appropriate contexts. In order to do that properly, a little review of recent history is appropriate.

In the late 1960's and early 1970's, Hawking (in conjunction with Roger Penrose and George Ellis) shook the scientific world with the development and publication of his space-time singularity theorems. Evidence had been building for about half a century in support of what had come to be known as "The Big Bang theory" (a somewhat inaccurate name which had been derisively coined by Sir Frederick Hoyle in 1949), but a substantial portion of the scientific community had been resisting "conversion". The metaphysical implications of a sudden beginning to the universe were very disturbing for those who had been proceeding on the assumptions of materialism, as it seemed to support Theism. As British Astrophysicist Sir Arthur Eddington once stated, "Philosophically, the notion of an abrupt beginning to the present order of Nature is repugnant to me."(4)

With the discovery of the Big Bang's microwave background radiation in 1964 (for which the discoverers earned a Nobel Prize), it was as if science had been teetering on a razor's edge. The resistance to the Big Bang had become quite an uphill battle, and the reconciliation of Einstein's Relativity with the motions of matter in the observed universe (which was addressed in the Hawking-Penrose Singularity Theorems) was the last set of puzzle pieces to make an overwhelming case. With the publication of the last of these, the case was effectively closed. Hawking and his colleagues had shown that when Einstein's General Relativity is applied to the observable universe, it shows the mother of all "singularities" when you trace it back in time -- an absolute beginning wherein time, space, matter and energy apparently began to exist from a single point. It then expanded outwardly from this point, creating space itself (!) as it proceeded. This was tough to accept for those who had presumed that the universe had existed eternally into the past and constructed worldviews based on that idea, but it was even harder to deny.

Although, as physicist Frank Tipler stated in a 2010 article, Hawking had provided "powerful valid theorems proving God's existence" (by way of proving that the universe began to exist:(5), Hawking somehow became opposed to the most natural conclusions one could derive from his work. It's not that he became an outright atheist, but he seemed to want to straddle the border between atheism and theism, perhaps to keep his options open. Since his 1988 book A Brief History of Time was somewhat difficult to read (one critic called it "the least-read bestseller of all time") and contained mutually contradictory metaphysical statements, not too many came away from it with a strong idea of Hawking's worldview. When asked by Shirley MacLaine whether he believed God had created the universe, Hawking replied simply "no", but look at these other quotes from him, either within the book or around that time:

Then we shall... be able to take part in the discussion of the question of why it is that we and the universe exist. If we find the answer to that, it would be the ultimate triumph of human reason - for then we would know the mind of God. (6)

And:

It is quite possible that God acts in ways that cannot be described by scientific laws, but in that case, one would just have to go by personal belief.(7)

When asked by a reporter whether he believed that science and Christianity were competing world views, Hawking replied:

...then Newton would not have discovered the law of gravity. [He knew that Newton had strong religious convictions.] (8)

Discussing the unification of quantum mechanics with an understanding of gravity:

Even if there is only one possible unified theory, it is just a set of rules and equations. What is it that breathes fire into the equations and makes a universe for them to describe? (9)

When commenting on quantum mechanics, Albert Einstein had stated that God "does not throw dice". (10) Hawking's response to that was:

God not only plays with dice, He sometimes throws them where they can't be seen. (11)

On the idea of a sub-omniscient God:

The idea that God might want to change His mind is an example of the fallacy, pointed out by St. Augustine, of imagining God as a being existing in time. Time is a property only of the universe that God created. Presumably, God knew what He intended when He set it up. (12)

And:

I thought I had left the question of the existence of a Supreme Being completely open. . . It would be perfectly consistent with all we know to say that there was a Being who was responsible for all the laws of physics. (13)

In perhaps the most revealing statement from A Brief History of Time, Hawking stated:

So long as the universe had a beginning, we could suppose it had a creator. But if the universe is really completely self-contained, having no boundary or edge, it would have neither beginning nor end: it would simply be. What place, then, for a creator? (14)

Notice that this notion doesn't attempt to answer the "ultimate metaphysical question" posed by Gottfried Wilhelm Leibniz a few hundred years ago, namely: "Why is there something instead of nothing?" We could grant Hawking's presupposition above — that the universe "just is"— and we would still have a profound mystery on our hands. Namely, "*why is* it?"

To paraphrase the atheist philosopher Richard Taylor, suppose we were walking along in the woods with someone and we came across a glowing ball, and we asked our companion "where did that come from?" If our companion answered "oh, that doesn't have an origin; it just is, that's all", we would rightly pronounce their answer as implausible, if not downright ludicrous. I think that most adults know instinctively that things are either caused to exist (we can imagine many examples of this), or they exist necessarily (far fewer things are in this category -- some philosophers would say it consists of only God; others might add "abstract objects" to the list). The requirement that causes must precede their effects (at least logically, if not also temporally) is known in philosophy as "The Causal Principle". As certainly as we would instinctively rule out the glowing ball as existing uncaused and necessarily, it's hard to imagine why we would qualify a larger object (such as a universe) as having these qualities. So why did Hawking "go there"?

In 1983, Hawking and UCSB physicist James Hartle developed what is now referred to as the Hartle-Hawking Quantum Gravity Model of the universe, in which the universe "has no beginning" because it

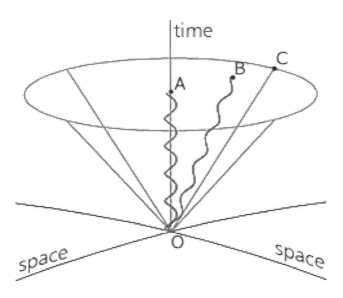

"has no boundary" where time began. What does this model look like? If we imagine a graph of the universe's expansion from an incredibly dense single point (hereinafter referred to as "the singularity") based on the standard Big Bang model, it would look like a cone. The point of the cone on this model represents the beginning, and the expansion of the universe is represented by the increasing width as we progress through time. What Hawking engineered in the Hartle-Hawking Model, however, was a theorized "rounding" of the pointed end of the cone such that it resembled a badminton birdie rather than a cone. He introduced the term "no-boundary" model (but I think "disguised boundary" would have been more accurate). The process Hawking used to achieve this end was to employ what he called "imaginary numbers". I'm glad he used this term, because I think it is an apt description.

"Imaginary numbers" have been used before by mathematicians to represent "time" in theoretical models involving its interaction with space. This is done to "grease" equations by treating it like a dimension of space, but the standard procedure is to interpret the imaginary numbers back to real numbers after the theoretical work is done. This is an important step, because contrary to the notion of "spacetime" popularized by science fiction, time is dissimilar to space in that it only goes in one direction – forward.

Many are confused on this point because Einstein began using the term "spacetime" in the early 1900's (following the lead of mathematician Hermann Minkowski), but neither Einstein, nor anyone else had ever proven that time could behave like space in the sense of going backwards (or in any direction besides forward). In order to explain observational evidence, Einstein had theorized that the passage of time was relative to reference frames and therefore rejected the notion of absolute simultaneity between objects moving at substantially different speeds. The great Dutch physicist Hendrik Lorentz, however, had an alternative viewpoint; the view that measuring devices (as opposed to time itself) were warped by high velocities. This seems to correspond to our common-sense apprehension of time more congruently than the idea that time can move differently in different reference frames such that there cannot be simultaneity. Only time and further experimentation will ultimately determine whether or not a Lorentzian interpretation of the data is warranted.

Going back to the Hartle-Hawking Model, the "imaginary numbers" they used are square roots of negative one (which don't exist in the real world). Again, in a massive digression from standard procedure, Hawking refused to interpret the imaginary numbers back into real ones! When one does so, the singularity re-appears. If your hokum detector is on, it should be buzzing by now!

It's important to note that Hawking had not substantially addressed any of the important published criticisms of the Hartle – Hawking model as of this writing, either prior to the release of The Grand Design, or in it. Nor is there any new science in it. Oddly enough, however, there is some slightly different language on the Hartle-Hawking theorem than that which was proposed in *A Brief History of Time*. In *The Grand Design*, the authors posit a beginning point for time on the south pole of their model:

> *The realization that time can behave like another direction of space means one can get rid of the problem of time having a beginning, in a similar way in which we got rid of the edge of the world. Suppose the beginning of the universe was like the South Pole of the earth, with degrees of latitude playing the role of time. As one moves north, the circles of constant latitude, representing the size of the universe, would expand. The universe would start as a point at the South Pole, but the South Pole is much like any other point. To ask what happened before the beginning of the universe would become a meaningless question, because there is nothing south of the South Pole. In this picture space-time has no boundary—the same laws of*

nature hold at the South Pole as in other places. (15)

In A Brief History of Time Hawking claimed that the Universe could just "be". Here we see the authors alluding to a "starting point" in a cyclically repetitive model, but trying to avoid its implications by definition ("To ask what happened before the beginning of the universe would become a meaningless question, because there is nothing south of the South Pole"). I think that the authors are trying to hide "the elephant in the room" (the causal principal) behind the notion that cause and effect generally need time within which to operate. "If time had not begun yet", the argument might go, "then how could God have operated to bring the universe into existence?" But God by definition is supernatural, so He's not subject to the general requirements within which creatures in the universe operate. He may very well be transcendent to time (if He made time, why not?). Beyond that, time is generally understood as the progression of moments within a changing system. God may have had the plan to bring the universe into existence from eternity-past in a sort of "metaphysical (changeless) time", and simply entered into interaction with time simultaneously with the creation of the universe. If it is, in fact, the question of the cause of the universe the authors mean to avoid here, it's hard to imagine a more meaningful one.

So what if we just assume for the sake of discussion that the "spacetime cone"'s end is rounded off? As philosopher/theologian William Lane Craig points out, we still don't have a past-eternal universe! Whether or not the theory uses the term "point", and no matter how rounded the end is, there is always a boundary between being and non-being. One can try to "hedge" this with ever-more-spherical models, but no matter what shape you dream up, it's not going to avoid having a beginning (or boundary). A rough analogy one could use to understand this point is a horse race; typically a single horse is the first out of the gate at the start of the race, but what if two or three horses get out first in an exact tie? In fact, what if the entire field gets out of the gate exactly simultaneously; do we have any less of a beginning? Of course not, and neither would we with the extremely speculative Hartle-Hawking model (if it were true).

Cosmologists use a term called "Cosmic Inflation" to describe what took place during what is known as "The Planck Time" (from 10^{-36} seconds after the Big Bang to sometime between 10^{-33} and 10^{-32} seconds after), when things were so small, dense and rapidly expanding that they are somewhat mysterious. But it seems to me that Hawking is exploiting this mysterious period to sell a viewpoint rather than to foment clarity. Relativity cannot adequately describe Cosmic Inflation because it is so close to the singularity (and thus so tiny) that it's a quantum–scale event; Relativity can only describe larger-scale phenomena. One can try to incorporate Quantum Physics in conjunction with Relativity (as Hawking attempts to do), but there is no consensus on which interpretation of QM (if any) is valid, much less how to reconcile it with Relativity, so it remains a mystery. That being said, scientists have a variety of theories as to what may have been occurring, and the majority involve the time-frame I specified above. Of course, anything involving a time frame is necessarily in time, so I think it's safe to say Hawking is in a tiny minority here.

Hawking pays homage to M-Theory (an 11-dimension harmonization of String Theories), but his colleagues don't seem to be in agreement with him that there can be "no boundary" between being and non-being afforded by M-Theory. Yet on page 134 of The Grand Design, Hawking claims that in the early universe, "there were effectively four dimensions of space and none of time" (purportedly due to time-warping from the incredible density). Notice that he uses the hedge word "effectively". He goes on to say that "time as we know it did not exist". Notice the hedge words "as we know it". Then he makes the leap to claiming we can model this mathematically and asserts that there was therefore no boundary, but as we saw before, his math uses "imaginary numbers" which he refuses to use responsibly. This is unprofessional legerdemain, in my opinion, and thoroughly fails to avoid a beginning.

So we can see that although Hawking has a tremendous mind for mathematics, certain other disciplines seem more difficult for him. This is a fairly common thing, as even the venerated Albert Einstein once remarked, "The man of science is a poor philosopher" (and Einstein himself was not immune to this, as much of his work presupposed the now-discredited philosophy of *Verificationism*).

So to recap, at some time adjacent to the publication of A Brief History of Time, Hawking began vacillating back and forth between public statements suggesting that the universe began to exist and that it was past-eternal. He has not consistently held that time had no beginning however; for example, in a 1996 book he co-authored with Roger Penrose called The Nature of Space and Time, he made the memorable quote, "Today virtually everyone agrees that the universe and time itself had a beginning at the Big Bang."(16) This idea of a finite past comports with what the vast majority of scientists and philosophers believe, as there is overwhelming evidence supporting it (we'll get more into that later). On this finite view, time, space, matter and energy suddenly came into existence, and prior to that, none of the above existed.

But wait a minute -- The Causal Principle requires there to be a cause for things that begin to exist! Since it is axiomatic that "from nothing, nothing comes", this raises the question "what caused the universe to come into existence?" Notice that the classical Judeo-Christian description of God; a timeless, spaceless, immaterial, spirit being with omniscience and immense power, would fit the bill.

Some would reply to that "this is not a scientific answer", but this answer bespeaks ignorance about the self-imposed limits of Science. Science describes nature. There are different opinions on where the boundaries of science lie (for more on this subject, do an internet search for "the demarcation problem"), but in every definition of "science", metaphysical ("meta" = "over" or "beyond") questions about what caused the universe are categorized as necessarily "pre-natural". They are governed by the rules of logical inference (a subcategory of

Philosophy) — and are not in the realm of science because they are logically prior to it. Properly construed, Science is necessarily agnostic (ignorant) on questions about origins of the metaphysical, or the physical. To assume that God is not a possibility, given what we know, then, would be a flagrant bias. Perhaps Hawking sensed this subconsciously and therefore "hedged his bets" in the past (of course I'm speculating), but if so, that has now certainly changed with the stance he has taken in The Grand Design.

The book does also feature a historical review of several important developments in science over the past few centuries, but aside from the aforementioned spin on the Hartle-Hawking model, the only things in it that seem truly new are mutually contradictory philosophical commitments (eg. Determinism, anti-realist Subjectivism) and a re-vamped nastiness towards spiritual matters).

When asked by Larry King what the most important point in The Grand Design is, Hawking answered "That science can explain the universe, and that we don't need God to explain why there is something rather than nothing or why the laws of nature are what they are." Again, notice that Hawking doesn't seem to realize where the boundary between physics and metaphysics is here (or he is pretending not to). Science only considers what the facts of nature might be. Questions of ultimate causes like "what caused nature to be" are deduced by logical inference and are firmly ensconced in the branch of philosophy known as "metaphysics". Science cannot explain _the source_ of the universe – it can only describe the universe and certain features thereof.

On page 135-136 of the book, the authors shamelessly abuse Richard Feynman's "Sum Over Histories" mathematical method for calculating the probability of a subatomic particle arriving at one point from another. Feynman had never intended this to represent actual multiple universes arising simultaneously, but rather as a tool to calculate historical probabilities of individual particle travel. Nevertheless, the authors not only peddle this absurd claim, but they assert that "in this view, the universe appeared spontaneously from nothing". (17) Once again, the causal principal is ignored.

Elsewhere in the book, they make the jarring claim that "because there is a law like gravity, the universe can and will create itself from nothing…". (18) Whoah – doesn't this put the "cart before the horse"?! I think it can be easily deduced that gravity (as well as the other fundamental forces) are features of the universe; not features that preceded the universe. If gravity preceded the universe, where did gravity come from? Indeed, Hawking himself makes the statement on page 83 of the book that "the laws of nature in our universe arose from the big bang". So which came first, the laws or the universe? And what happened to the universe appearing "spontaneously from nothing"? Geez – pick a story and stick with it, Steve - O!

To illustrate the incoherence of the assertion to Larry King quoted above (the notion that the universe arose from "nothing"), let's take a look at the concept of "nothing" for a minute. The true philosophical description of nothing is "non-being". I believe it was Aristotle who described nothing as being "what rocks dream about" (Aristotle was a theist, so he was speaking of the physical world -- God is non-physical, so this was not meant to imply atheism). Keep this classical description of true "nothingness" in mind as we proceed forward.

"Nothing", properly understood, has no matter, energy, time, or space – it can have no physical properties such as laws, or "instability" (as certain pseudo-philosophers and pseudo-scientists sometimes claim). Yet Hawking, in claiming that the universe could have arisen from "nothing" is equivocating between two different definitions of nothing.

In Quantum Physics, the term "nothing" is sometimes sloppily used to describe a fluctuating quantum field; that is, a space with a rich physical structure seething with energy. This is not "nothing" in the classical sense of the term (because it has space, matter, energy and is in time), but in recent years it has become fashionable for intellectually dishonest people to conflate these two concepts in order to support atheism. The so-called "New Atheists" (who happen to all be terrible philosophers) come to mind. In these fluctuating quantum fields mentioned above, there seem to be quantum particles briefly disappearing and appearing – but it's far from clear that they actually come into existence and cease to exist.

Quantum physicists differ on their interpretation of these phenomena. There are at least ten different physical interpretations of quantum phenomena, and new theories are being proposed due to the discoveries at the CERN super-collider as I write this. Nobody knows yet which of these models (if any) is the correct one. Frankly, there are problems with all of them, including the Sum-Over-Histories and Many-Worlds variants that Hawking seems to favor (within an M-Theory narrative). Nevertheless, if we grant for the sake of discussion that particles can truly come into existence spontaneously from what these authors call "nothing" (19), but which is actually a fluctuating quantum field, does it help them? Nope! A grand total of 0 (zero) quantum interpretations show that you get something from true nothing. The situation described above as "nothing" (the quantum vacuum), is actually within time and space, has a rich physical structure, and so is not a true nothing. This claim is simply linguistic slight-of-hand. The fact that Hawking has abandoned the ongoing discussion and thrown in with the "new atheist" types that peddle this type of shystery is rather disgraceful for a man who once sat in Isaac Newton's chair at Cambridge.

Because abstract concepts can be slippery, bear with me while I address several of the more important claims the authors make once again in different wording:

A) miracles are impossible (20).

B) there is no free will (everything is pre-determined) (21), and

C) objective reality doesn't exist (all reality is observer-dependent) (22).

On item A), as I alluded to earlier in this chapter, Hawking seems to have bought into (or is otherwise beholden to) a fairly common error. This error is in assuming that the definition of "Science" (i.e.; methods of determining facts about the natural world that, for the sake of methodological purity, presuppose that nature is all that exists) extends to all of ontic reality (all which actually DOES exist, including, but not limited to, nature).

In other words, instead of recognizing that the empirical rules of science make it necessarily incomplete (because by definition, it can form no metaphysical opinions), they blunder forward on the assumption that it includes everything. This confusion becomes obvious when somebody tries to shut down discussions of things like intelligent design by saying "it's not science!" One can readily admit that not all possible explanations of many things (whether abstract, material or immaterial) are "science", but that does not mean much because science is a very limited discipline. What the person frequently intends to express when they say things like this is: "it's not logical!"

But of course, logic is a far broader discipline than narrow science, so this is a misuse of the term "science".

The term "science" used to be simply the search for truth, as great minds of the past such as Newton, Boyle and Kepler used it, but the term has evolved in the past several hundred years. Again, the common modern definition does not allow for the consideration of the supernatural, under any circumstances. If everything in life were fair, this change would have added an asterisk/notation onto every deduction thereafter in science, much like sports records have for marks achieved under different rules. The appurtenant notation could say something like: *Post-"Naturalistic Assumptions".

Many otherwise fairly educated folks (including some scientists!) don't even know this limitation about the term, and it results in the comical spectre of some of them actually arguing that they believe in "nothing but science". "Really?" one could answer. "No love, no memories, no poetry, no fun; nothing but what you can prove scientifically? Hypothetically speaking, a 300-foot-tall Yahweh could suddenly appear in front of an assembly of these folks in the lab, playing bass and singing The HalleluJah Chorus with Jesus at His side on keyboard and The Holy Ghost on drums, and if they were consistent, they would have to deny that they are seeing it because "it's not science" (props to Tom Wolfe for the metaphor). I guess it would probably be written off as a hallucination.

As strange as it seems, the sustained use of the scientific method (the seeds of which, ironically, came from the Bible) has led to the common misunderstanding that the supernatural cannot possibly exist. Most professional thinkers (Philosophers) understand that the supernatural cannot be ruled out by such feeble reasoning, however, as "absence of evidence does not equal evidence of absence", among other things.

If, as Christopher Hitchens used to like to say, "we barely know what we don't know", then how utterly arrogant it would be to make such a universally negative claim? If there were no testimony whatsoever among humanity of supernatural experience, we still would not have an adequate sample size for this sort of statement; how much less so when the vast majority of human beings who have existed (including Hawking's Christian wife) claim the opposite? Drawing atheistic ontological conclusions from a man-made methodology would be very foolish indeed. Mankind's tenancy on the earth has been barely the blink of an eye compared to the age of the universe. What if God is subtle, and obvious miracles are just rare? Hawking and Mlodonow, however, seem to have bought into this notion wholesale.

Regarding B) above, it's self-refuting! If there is no free will, then Hawking and Mlodonow didn't write this book on the basis of reason, but rather simply because their internal chemistry compelled them to. The arrangement of that internal chemistry, on this viewpoint, was nothing more than an accident. For all we know, their internal chemistry could have compelled them to write stultifying nonsense and pass it off as a scientific book (whoops – self-referential echo chamber! ;^). On this viewpoint then, nothing in it can be taken seriously. How this one got past the editor, I'll never figure out.

Regarding C) above, once again, this is relativism. They use the illustration of a goldfish looking out of its bowl and seeing a distorted world, as contrasted with humans looking into the bowl at the fish.

http://www.wpclipart.com

In using the phrases "model-dependent reality" or "observer-dependent reality" however, the authors reveal bias and possibly, confusion. Nearly everyone knows that the perspective of any creature can be distorted, and is therefore "subjective". But consider the picture above; is it the "reality" that is observer-dependent (or model-dependent), or is it the perspective? Perspectives are certainly observer dependent – in the case above, both the cat and the fish see a distorted image of one another -- but reality is not (otherwise there would have been no reality prior to the first creature, but who believes that?).

The law of non-contradiction says that for any given proposition "P", the contradictory proposition "not P" cannot simultaneously be true. Is the cat's perspective "C" (which we can see is warped in a convex fashion by the glass) true, the goldfish's "G" (which we see is warped in a concave fashion by the glass), or neither? Since they don't match, if the cat's is true, then that of the goldfish must be false. If that of the goldfish is true, then the cat's must be false. We tend to think that our human viewpoint is correct, but it's possible that something we're unaware of is warping our perspective as well.

Now if God is omniscient, His perspective is true, understands all subjective viewpoints, and meets the definition of "objective", even if all other opinions are subjective. Hawking and Mlodonow seem to want to smuggle in the presupposition that there is no objective reality, and hence, no God. As I have noticed time and time again, their worldview seems to be steered by what they want to believe, rather than being steered by the truth into the best inference. I see no reason to accept either their stated or implied worldviews based on the incoherent flailings in this book.

A book called *A Universe From Nothing* making claims similar to Hawking's was recently released by an atheist physicist named Lawrence Krauss. A brief word on that seems warranted: I've read several reviews, and listened to several podcasts critiquing it, and predictably, he follows the same pattern set by Hawking of dancing back and forth between different definitions of "nothing" ("non-being" vs. a fluctuating quantum field that "might as well be nothing"). Also predictably, he makes freshman philosophical mistakes while bad-mouthing philosophy and theology frequently throughout the book. The reviewers (Dr. David Albert and Dr. William Lane Craig) were not impressed. In a series of debates/discussions in Australia with William Lane Craig this year (2013), Krauss exhibited extremely childlike behavior; interrupting, ringing a "Dr. Craig BS Buzzer" he had brought with him every time he heard something he didn't like, contradicting his own previous statements (and even some made during the series of debates!), and generally behaving like a boorish man-child.

Apparently Krauss felt slighted by Dr. Craig's dismantling of his amateurish arguments in their previous debate (and communications) thereafter, and this was his way of attempting to "even the score". Having reviewed the video, I don't think anyone besides the sycophants were impressed. Krauss offered nothing new, and made the same self-refuting mistake of engaging in philosophy to attempt to "dis" philosophy (as if Science can be done without philosophy). Dr. Craig is a brilliant man, but what causes him to win these debates with atheists year-after-year (for well over two decades now) is not self-promotion or stubbornness – it's because he is on the side of truth. It would be nice to detect that motivation from atheists now and again.

In Science, predictability tells us a great deal about the nature of matter and energy. In disciplines like Theology, Philosophy, Psychology and Sociology, predictability tells us a great deal about the nature of people. Some of the laws of nature we notice in Science, like inertia, seem to have corollaries in creaturely behavior. Various types of animals, for example, will stampede over a cliff for no more reason than that they assume that the leaders (and consequently, the pack) are heading in a good direction. It behooves us all to pay close attention where we can, and resist parallel phenomena with regard to our human "leaders".

SUMMARY

"Gold and diamonds cast a spell, it's not for me I know it well
The treasures that I seek are waiting on the other side
There's more that I can measure in the treasure of the love that I can find
And though it's always been with me, I must tear down the Wall and let it be
All I am, and all that I was ever meant to be, in harmony
Shining true and smiling back at all who wait to cross
THERE IS NO LOSS"

~from *"The Wall"*, by Kansas

Public Domain / NASA/JPL-Caltech/Univ. of Ariz.

Let's review what we've gone over in a summarized form:

- The scientific view is virtually unanimous that time, space, matter and energy came into existence suddenly in a tremendous "explosion" from a single location at a finite point in the past. This expansion is still continuing, and both the sudden beginning and the continuing expansion of the universe were accurately described by six different Biblical authors.

- The scientific view is virtually unanimous that there is an incredible, overwhelming appearance that the universe was fine-tuned to support life. The scientific term for this is "The Anthropic Principle".

- The common scientific view of the "hardware of life" is, as Richard Dawkins puts it, "the study of complicated things that give the appearance of having been designed for a purpose." (The Blind Watchmaker, 1986). Studies at the cellular level show that for life to have developed by chance is far, far beyond mathematically impossible and they evince a distinct impression of design. This impression is so overwhelming that, as Francis Crick stated: "Biologists must constantly keep in mind that what they see was not designed, but rather evolved." [*What Mad Pursuit* (1988)]

- There are hundreds of quadrillions of communicating computers in our bodies. The odds against even the simplest cell forming by chance are far, far beyond what is mathematically possible. The common scientific view of the information content in the genetic "software of life" is, as Francis Crick and Robert Shapiro put it, tantamount to "a miracle".

- We each experience the subjective phenomenon of personal consciousness and self-awareness, which science has no good explanation for, and which suggests that not only are we more than random chemical interactions, but that we have souls.

- The vast majority of human beings agree that there are objective moral values in the universe. These objective moral values must have been grounded in a transcendent mind, otherwise they are not objective, but subjective, and are dependent solely on human opinion.

- The evidence that Jesus Christ was resurrected from the dead has multiple, independent, early attestation from individuals and groups, many of whom refused to recant their faith even while suffering tremendous persecution and martyrdom.

- The Shroud of Turin has the imprint of a man that suffered the exact same violence as Jesus Christ per the description in the Bible. The carbon dating that suggested a 13th century generation of The Shroud has been ruled out as a valid test due to contamination of the Shroud fibers.

The only possible explanation for the image on the Shroud is an incredibly intense yet subtle radiation from the body over which it was draped.

- Recent attempts by highly-respected physicists to formulate a something-from-nothing hypothesis in order to avoid the implications of the Big Bang have failed miserably, and thus reconfirm our certainty that our universe had a supernatural beginning. As Alexander Vilenkin stated at Stephen Hawking's 70th birthday party (probably to Hawking's dismay) in January 2012: "All the evidence we have says that the universe had a beginning."

I am confident that the only possible logical conclusion that can be reached from this evidence is that Jesus Christ is the Son of God. If you agree, and would like to accept Jesus Christ as your personal Lord and Savior, say a prayer like this:

"Heavenly Father, please forgive me of my sins. I accept the payment that was given by your Son on my behalf, and receive Him as my Lord and Savior. Thank you for allowing me to be your child. I commit my life to you, and sharing the good news about your love. Amen!"

If you have done so, I congratulate you and welcome you into the Kingdom of God. <><

Marq Spusta 'Bliss Bug', from:
http://postersandprints.wordpress.com/page/2/

References

CHAPTER ONE

1) William Lane Craig, Reasonable Faith, third edition (Crossway), p. 106.

2) On the Infinite," in Philosophy of Mathematics, ed. Paul Benacerraf and Hilary Putnam (Englewood Cliffs, NJ: Prentice-Hall, 1964), p. 151.

3) Fred Hoyle, From Stonehenge to Modern Cosmology (San Francisco: W.H. Freeman, 1972), p. 36.

4) Anthony Kenny, The Five Ways: St. Thomas Aquinas' Proofs of God's Existence (New York: Schocken Books, 1969), p. 66.

5) The Kalam Cosmological Argument (New York: Harper & Row, 1979), page 63.

6) Many Worlds in One (New York: Hill and Wang, 2006), p.176.

7) Old Earth Creationism: Setting the Record Straight, Jon W. Greene Reasons to Believe - Seattle Area Chapter News and Views August 2006).

8) Thomas H. Maugh, II (April 24, 1992). "Relics of Big Bang, Seen for First Time". Los Angeles Times: pp. A1, A30.

9) The Los Angeles Times, Saturday 2nd May 1992.

10) Smoot, George, Wrinkles in Time, 2007 edition , cover.

11) Greenstein, G. 1988. The Symbiotic Universe. New York: William Morrow, p.27.

12) Heeren, F. 1995. Show Me God. Wheeling, IL, Searchlight Publications, p. 233.

13) Margenau, H and R.A. Varghese, ed. 1992. Cosmos, Bios, and Theos. La Salle, IL, Open Court, p. 83.

14) Penrose, R. 1992. A Brief History of Time (movie). Burbank, CA, Paramount Pictures, Inc.

15) Jastrow, R. 1978. God and the Astronomers. New York, W.W. Norton, p. 116.

16) Tipler, F.J. 1994. The Physics Of Immortality. New York, Doubleday, Preface.

17) Gannes, S. October 13, 1986. Fortune. p. 57

18) Heeren, F. 1995. Show Me God. Wheeling, IL, Searchlight Publications, p. 166-167.

19) Margenau, H. and R. A. Varghese, eds. Cosmos, Bios, Theos: Scientists Reflect on Science, God, and the Origins of the Universe, Life, and Homo Sapiens (Open Court Pub. Co., La Salle, IL, 1992).

20) McIver, T. 1986. Ancient Tales and Space-Age Myths of Creationist Evangelism. The Skeptical Inquirer 10:258-276.

21) McIver, T. 1986. Ancient Tales and Space-Age Myths of Creationist Evangelism. The Skeptical Inquirer 10:258-276.

CHAPTER TWO

1) Most of the source references may be found in The Creator and the Cosmos, 3rd edition by Hugh Ross (Colorado Springs, CO: NavPress, 2001), pp. 145-157, 245-248. Additional references are listed below:

1. John Leslie, editor, Physical Cosmology and Philosophy (New York: Macmillan, 1990), pp. 121-180.

2. Weihsueh A. Chiu, Nickolay Y. Gneden and Jeremiah P. Ostriker, "The Expected Mass Function for Low-Mass Galaxies in a Cold Dark Matter Cosmology: Is There a Problem?" Astrophysical Journal, 563 (2001), pp. 21-27.

3. Martin Elvis, Massimo Marengo, and Margarita Karovska, "Smoking Quasars: A New Source for Cosmic Dust," Astrophysical Journal Letters, 567 (2002), pp. L107-L110.

4. Martin White and C. S. Kochanek, "Constraints on the Long-Range Properties of Gravity from Weak Gravitational Lensing," Astrophysical Journal, 560 (2001), pp. 539-543.

5. P. P. Avelino and C. J. A. P. Martins, "A Supernova Brane Scan," Astrophysical Journal, 565 (2002), pp. 661-667.

6. P. deBernardis, et al, "Multiple Peaks in the Angular Power Spectrum of the Cosmic Microwave Background: Significance and Consequences for Cosmology," Astrophysical Journal, 564 (2002), pp. 559-566.

   A. T. Lee, et al, "A High Spatial Resolution Analysis of the MAXIMA-1 Cosmic

Microwave Background Anisotropy Data," Astrophysical Journal Letters, 561 (2001), pp. L1-L5.

7. R. Stompor, et al, "Cosmological Implications of MAXIMA-1 High-Resolution Cosmic Microwave Background Anisotropy Measurement," Astrophysical Journal Letters, 561 (2001), pp. L7-L10.

8. Andrew Watson, "Cosmic Ripples Confirm Universe Speeding Up," Science, 295 (2002), pp. 2341-2343.

9. Anthony Aguirre, Joop Schaye, and Eliot Quataert, "Problems for Modified Forest?"?Newtonian Dynamics in Clusters and the Ly Astrophysical Journal, 561 (2001), pp. 550-558.

10. Chris Blake and Jasper Wall, "A Velocity Dipole in the Distribution of

Radio Galaxies," Nature, 416 (2002), pp. 150-152.

11. G. Efstathiou, et al, "Evidence for a Non-Zero L and a Low Matter Density from a Combined Analysis of the 2dF Galaxy Redshift Survey and Cosmic Microwave Background Anisotropies," Monthly Notices of the Royal Astronomical Society, 330 (2002), pp. L29-L35.

12. Susana J. Landau and Hector Vucetich, "Testing Theories That Predict Time Variation of Fundamental Constants, " Astrophysical Journal, 570 (2002), pp. 463-469.

13. Renyue Cen, "Why Are There Dwarf Spheroidal Galaxies?" Astrophysical Journal Letters, 549 (2001), pp. L195-L198.

14. Brandon Carter, "Energy Dominance and the Hawking-Ellis Vacuum Conservation Theorem," a

contribution to Stephen Hawking's 60th birthday workshop on the Future of Theoretical Physics and Cosmology, Cambridge, UK, January, 2002, arXiv:gr-qc/0205010v1, May 2, 2002.

15. Joseph F. Hennawi and Jeremiah P. Ostriker, "Observational Constraints on the Self-Interacting Dark Matter Scenario and the Growth of Supermassive Black Holes," Astrophysical Journal, 572 (2002), pp. 41-54.

16. Robert Brandenberger, Brandon Carter, and Anne-Christine Davis, "Microwave Background Constraints on Decaying Defects," Physics Letters B, 534 (2002), pp. 1-7.

17. Lawrence M. Krauss, "The End of the Age Problem, and the Case for a Cosmological Constant Revisited," Astrophysical Journal, 501 (1998), pp. 461-466.

18.?Q. R. Ahmad, et al, "Measurement of the Rate of e p + p???+ d + e-Interactions Produced by 8B Solar Neutrinos at the Sudbury Neutrino Observatory," Physical Review Letters, 87 (2001), id. 071301.

19.R. E. Davies and R. H. Koch, "All the Observed Universe Has Contributed to Life," Philosophical Transactions of the Royal Society, 334B (1991), pp. 391-403.

20.George F. R. Ellis, "The Anthropic Principle: Laws and Environments," in The Anthropic Principle, edited by F. Bertola and U. Curi (New York: Cambridge University Press, 1993), p. 30.

21.H. R. Marston, S. H. Allen, and S. L. Swaby, "Iron Metabolism in Copper-Deficient Rats," British Journal of Nutrition, 25 (1971), pp. 15-30.

22.K. W. J. Wahle and N. T. Davies, "Effect of Dietary Copper Deficiency in the Rat on Fatty Acid Composition of Adipose Tissue and Desaturase Activity of Liver Microsomes," British Journal of Nutrition, 34 (1975), pp. 105-112;.

23. Walter Mertz, "The Newer Essential Trace Elements, Chromium, Tin, Vanadium, Nickel, and Silicon," Proceedings of the Nutrition Society, 33 (1974), pp. 307-313.

24. Bruno Leibundgut, "Cosmological Implications from Observations of Type Ia Supernovae," Annual Reviews of Astronomy and Astrophysics, 39 (2001), pp. 67-98.

25. C. L. Bennett, et al, "First Year Wilkinson Microwave Anisotropy Probe (WMAP) Observations, Preliminary Maps, and Basic Results," Astrophysical Journal Supplement, 148 (2003), pp. 1-27.

26. G. Hinshaw, et al, ""First Year Wilkinson Microwave Anisotropy

Probe (WMAP) Observations: Angular Power Spectrum," Astrophysical Journal Supplement, 148 (2003), pp. 135-159.

A. Balbi, et al, "Probing Dark Energy with the Cosmic Microwave Background: Projected Constraints from the Wilkinson Microwave Anisotropy Probe and Planck," Astrophysical Journal Letters, 588 (2003), pp. L5-L8.

27. Vikhlinin, et al, "Cosmological Constraints from the Evolution of the Cluster Baryon Mass Function at z = 0.5," Astrophysical Journal, 590 (2003), pp. 15-25.

28. Frank Thim, et al, "The Cepheid Distance to NGC 5236 (M83) with the ESO Very Large Telescope,"

Astrophysical Journal, 590 (2003), pp. 256-270.

29. Kazuhide Ichikawa and M. Kawasaki, "Constraining the Variation of the Coupling Constants with Big Bang Nucleosynthesis," Physical Review D, 65 (2002), id 123511.

30. Eubino-Martin José Alberto, et al, "First Results from the Very Small Array-IV. Cosmological Parameter Estimation," Monthly Notices of the Royal Astronomical Society, 341 (2003), pp. 1084-1092.

31. ?Takuji Tsujimoto and Toshikazu Shigeyama, "Star Formation History of Centauri Imprinted in Elemental Abundance Patterns," Astrophysical Journal, 590 (2003), pp. 803-808.

32. Santi Cassissi, Maurizio Salaris, and Alan W. Irwin, "The Initial Helium Content of Galactic Globular Cluster Stars from the R-Parameter: Comparison with the Cosmic

Microwave Background Constraint," Astrophysical Journal, 588 (2003), pp. 862-870.

33. Naoki Yoshida, et al, "Early Structure Formation and Reionization in a Warm Dark Matter Cosmology," Astrophysical Journal Letters, 591 (2003), pp. L1-L4.

34. Robert R. Caldwell, et al, "Early Quintessence in Light of the Wilkinson Microwave Anisotropy Probe," Astrophysical Journal Letters, 591 (2003), pp. L75-L78.

35. V. Luridiana, et al, "The Effect of Collisional Enhancement of Balmer Lines on the Determination of the Primordial Helium Abundance," Astrophysical Journal, 592 (20030, pp. 846-865.

36. Y. Jack Ng, W. A. Christiansen, and H. van Dam, "Probing Planck-Scale Physics with Extragalactic Sources?"

Astrophysical Journal Letters, 591 (2003), pp. L87-L89.

37. J. L. Sievers, et al, "Cosmological Parameters from Cosmic Background Imager Observations and Comparisons with BOOMERANG, DASI, and MAXIMA," Astrophysical Journal, 591 (2003), pp. 599-622.

38. R. Scranton, et al, "Physical Evidence for Dark Energy," submitted July 20, 2003 to Physical Review Letters, http://xxx.lanl.gov/abs/astro-ph/0307335.

39. Pablo Fosalba, Enrique Gaztanaga, and Francisco Castander, "Detection of the Integrated Sachs-Wolfe and Sunyaev-Zeldovich Effects from the Cosmic Microwave Background-Galaxy Correlation." Astrophysical Journal Letters, 597 (2003), pp. L89-L92.

40. M. R. Nolta, et al, "First Year Wilkinson Anistropy Probe (WMAP)

Observations: Dark Energy Induced Correlation with Radio Sources," submitted May 7, 2003 to Astrophysical Journal, http://xxx.lanl.gov/abs/astro-ph/0305097.

41. Stephen Boughn and Robert Crittenden, "A Correlation Between the Cosmic Microwave Background and Large-Scale Structure in the Universe," Nature, 427 (2004), pp. 45-47.

42. T. Jacobson, S. Liberati, and D. Mattingly, "A Strong Astrophysical Constraint on the Violation of Special Relativity by Quantum Gravity," Nature, 424 (2003), pp. 1019-1021.

43. Sean Carroll, "Quantum Gravity: An Astrophysical Constraint," Nature, 424 (2003), pp. 1007-1008.

44. D. J. Fixsen, "The Spectrum of the Cosmic Microwave Background Anisotropy from the Combined COBE

FIRAS and WMAP Observations," Astrophysical Journal Letters, 594 (2003), pp. L67-L70.

45. John L. Tonry, et al, "Cosmological Results from High-z Supernovae," Astrophysical Journal, 594 (2003), pp. 1-24.

46. Jean-Pierre Luminet, et al, "Dodecahedral Space Topology as an Explanation for Weak-Angle Temperature Correlations in the Cosmic Microwave Background," Nature, 425 (2003), pp. 593-595.

47. George F. R. Ellis, "The Shape of the Universe," Nature, 425 (2003), pp. 566-567.

48. Charles Seife, "Polyhedral Model Gives the Universe an Unexpected Twist," Science, 302 (2003), p. 209.

49. Neil J. Cornish, et al, "Constraining the Topology of the Universe," astro-

ph/0310233, submitted to Physical Review Letters, 2003.

50. David Kirkman, et al, "The Cosmological Baryon Density from the Deuterium-to-Hydrogen Ratio in QSO Absorption Systems: D/H Toward Q1243+3047," Astrophysical Journal Supplement, 149 (2003), pp. 1-28.

51. Jeremiah P. Ostriker, et al, "The Probability Distribution Function of Light in the Universe: Results from Hydrodynamic Simulations," Astrophysical Journal, 597 (2003), pp. 1-8.

52. M. Tegmark, et al, "Cosmological Parameters from SDSS and WMAP," preprint, 2003 posted at http://xxx.lanl.gov/abs/astro-ph/0310723.

53. Wolfram Freudling, Michael R. Corbin, and Kirk T. Korista, "Iron Emission in z ~ 6 QSOs," Astrophysical

Journal Letters, 587 (2003), pp. L67-L70.

54. Lennox L. Cowie and Antoinette Songaila, "The inconstant constant?" Nature 428 (2004), pp. 132-133.

55. H. Chand, et al., "Probing the cosmological variation of the fine-structure constant: Results based on VLT-UVES sample," Astronomy and Astrophysics, 417 (2004), pp. 853-871.

56. Thibault Damous and Freeman Dyson, "The Oklo bound on the time variation of the fine-structure constant revisited," Nuclear Physics B, 480 (1996), pp. 37-54.

57. Anton M. Koekemoer, et al, "A Possible New Population of Sources with Extreme X-Ray/Optical Ratios," Astrophysical Journal Letters, 600 (2004), pp. L123-L126.

58. Henry C. Ferguson, et al, "The Size Evolution of High-Redshift Galaxies," Astrophysical Journal, 600 (2004), pp. L107-L110.

59. Charles Seife, "Light from Most-Distant Supernovae Shows Dark Energy Stays the Course," Science, 303 (2004), p. 1271.

60. Jonathan C. Tan and Christopher F. McKee, "The Formation of the First Stars. I. Mass Infall Rates, Accretion Disk Structure, and Protostellar Evolution," Astrophysical Journal, 603 (2004), pp. 383-400.

61. Charles Seife, "Galactic Stripling Gives a Glimpse of the Universe's Raw Youth," Science, 303 (2004), p. 1597.

62. Alan Heavens, et al, "The Star Formation History of the Universe from the Stellar Populations of Nearby Galaxies," Nature, 428 (2004), pp. 625-627.

63. Pavel D. Naselsky, et al, "Primordial Magnetic Field and Non-Gaussianity of the One-Year Wilkinson Microwave Anisotropy Probe Data," Astrophysical Journal, 615 (2004), pp. 45-54.

64. Gang Chen, et al, "Looking for Cosmological Alfvén Waves in Wilkinson Microwave Anisotropy Probe Data," Astrophysical Journal, 611 (2004), pp. 655-659.

65. Tommaso Treu and Léon V. E. Koopmans, "Massive Dark Matter Halos and Evolution of Early-Type Galaxies to z = 1," Astrophysical Journal, 611 (2004), pp. 739-760.

66. Aubert, et al (the BaBar Collaboration), "Observations of Direct CP Violation in B0® K+pi-Decays," preprint, August, 2004, high energy physics - experiment.

67. Mark Peplow, "The Bs Have It," Nature, 430 (2004), p. 739.

68. Peter Bond, "Hubble's Long View," Astronomy & Geophysics, volume 45, issue 3, June 2004, p. 328.

    A. C. S. Readhead, et al, "Polarization Observations with the Cosmic Background Imager," Science, 306 (2004), pp. 836-844.

69. Nickolay Y. Gneidin, "Reionization, Sloan, and WMAP: Is the Picture Consistent?" Astrophysical Journal, 610 (2004), pp. 9-13.

70. Amr A. El-Zant, et al, "Flat-Cored Dark Matter in Cuspy Clusters of Galaxies," Astrophysical Journal Letters, 607 (2004), pp. L75-L78.

71. J. R. Lin, S. N. Zhang, and T. P. Li, "Gamma-Ray Bursts Are Produced Predominantly in the Early Universe," Astrophysical Journal, 605 (2004), pp. 819-822.

72. Timothy P. Ashenfelter and Grant J. Mathews, "The Fine-Structure Constant as a Probe of Chemical Evolution and Asymptotic Giant Branch Nucleosynthesis in Damped Lya Systems," Astrophysical Journal, 615 (2004), pp. 82-97.

73. Naoki Yoshida, Volker Bromm, and Lars Hernquist,, "The Era of Massive Population III Stars: Cosmological Implications and Self-Termination," The Astrophysical Journal, 605, (2004), pp. 579-590.

74. YesheFenner, Jason X. Prochaska and Brad K. Gibson, "Constraints on Early Nucleosynthesis from the Abundance Pattern of a Damped Ly_ System at z = 2.626," The Astrophysical Journal, 606 (2004), pp. 116-125.

75. Andreas Heithausen,, "Molecular Hydrogen as Baryonic Dark Matter," The Astrophysical Journal Letters, 606 (2004), pp. L13-L15.

76. Douglas Clowe, Anthony Gonzalez, and Maxim Markevitch, "Weak-Lensing Mass Reconstruction of the Interacting Cluster IE 0657-558: Direct Evidence for the Existence of Dark Matter," Astrophysical Journal, 604 (2004), pp. 596-603.

77. Sean T. Prigge, et al, "Dioxygen Binds End-On to Mononuclear Copper in a Precatalytic Enzyme Complex," Science, 304 (2004), pp. 864-867.

78. H. Jakubowski, Biochemistry: Chapter 8: Oxidative-Phosphorylation, A: The Chemistry of Dioxygen, November 17, 2005, http://employees.csbsju.edu/hjakubowski/classes/ch331/oxphos/oldioxygenchem.html. Accessed 02/06/06.

79. Robert H. Abeles, Perry A. Frey, and William P. Jencks, Biochemistry (Boston: Jones and Bartlett, 1992), pp. 655-673.

80. P. Caresia, S. Matarrese, and L. Moscardini, "Constraints on Extended Quintessence from High-Redshift Supernovae," Astrophysical Journal, 605 (2004), pp. 21-28.

81. AmrA. El-Zant, et al, "Flat-Cored Dark Matter in Cuspy Clusters of Galaxies," Astrophysical Journal Letters, 607 (2004), pp. L75-L78.

82. Kyu-Hyun Chae, et al, "Constraints on Scalar-Field Dark Energy from the Cosmic Lens All-Sky Survey Gravitational Lens Statistics," Astrophysical Journal Letters, 607 (2004), pp. L71-74.

83. Max Tegmark, et al, "The Three-Dimensional Power Spectrum of Galaxies From the Sloan Digital Sky Survey," Astrophysical Journal, 606 (2004), pp. 702-740.

84. Adrian C. Pope, et al, "Cosmological Parameters from Eigenmode Analysis of Sloan Digital Sky Survey Galaxy

Redshifts," Astrophysical Journal, 607 (2004), pp. 655-660.

85. YunWang and Pia Mukherjee, "Model-Independent Constraints on Dark Energy Density from Flux-Averaging Analysis of Type Ia Supernova Data," Astrophysical Journal, 606 (2004), pp. 654-663.

86. Adam G. Riess, et al, "Type Ia Supernova Discoveries at z>1 from the Hubble Space Telescope: Evidence for Past Deceleration and Constraints on Dark Energy Evolution," Astrophysical Journal, 607 (2004), pp. 665-687.

A. Kashlinsky, et al, "Detecting Population III Stars Through Observations of Near-Infrared Cosmic Infrared Background Anisotropies," Astrophysical Journal, 608 (2004), pp. 1-9.

383

87. Nickolay Y. Gneidin, "Reionization, Sloan, and WMAP: Is the Picture Consistent?" Astrophysical Journal, 610 (2004), pp. 9-13.

88. Paul Martin and Luis C. Ho, "A Population of Massive Globular Clusters in NGC 5128," Astrophysical Journal, 610 (2004), pp. 233-246.

89. L. Pasquini, et al, "Beryllium in Turnoff Stars of NGC6397: Early Galaxy Spallation Cosmochronology and Cluster Formation," Astronomy and Astrophysics, in press, 2004.

90. Peter Bond, "Hubble's Long View," Astronomy & Geophysics, volume 45, issue 3, June 2004, p. 328.

91. T. Harko and K. S. Cheng, "Time Delay of Photons of Different Energies in Multidimensional Cosmological Models," Astrophysical Journal, 611 (2004), pp. 633-641.

92.H. Stairs, S. E. Thorsett, and Z. Arzoumanian, "Measurement of Gravitational Soin-Orbit Coupling in a Binary Pulsar System," Physical Review Letters, 93 (2004), id. 141101.

93.Daniel B. Zucker, et al, "Andromeda IX. A New Dwarf Speroidal Satellite of M31," Astrophysical Journal Letters, 612 (2004), pp. L121-L124.

94.Patrick Henry, "X-Ray Temperatures for the Extended Medium-Sensitivity Survey High-Redshift Cluster Sample: Constraints on Cosmology and the Dark Energy Equation of State," Astrophysical Journal, 609 (2004), pp. 603-616.

95.S. W. Allen, et al, "Constraints on Dark Energy from Chandra Observations of the Largest Relaxed Galaxy Clusters," Monthly Notices of the Royal Astronomical Society, 353 (2004), pp. 457-467.

96. Ruth A. Daly and S. G. Djorgovski, "Direct Determination of the Kinematics of the Universe and Properties of the Dark Energy as Functions of Redshift," Astrophysical Journal, 612 (2004), pp. 652-659.

97. Ruth A. Daly and S. G. Djorgovski, "A Model-Independent Determination of the Expansion and Acceleration Rates of the Universe as a Function of Redshift and Constraints on Dark Energy," Astrophysical Journal 597 (2003), pp. 9-20.

98. E. Peik, et al, "Limit on the Present Temporal Variation of the Fine Structure Constant," Physical Review Letters, 93 (2004), id # 170801.

99. Ciufolini and E. C. Pavils, "A Confirmation of the General Relativistic Prediction of the Lense-Thirring Effect," Nature, 431 (2004), pp. 958-960.

100.   Timothy P. Ashenfelter and Grant J. Mathews, "The Fine-Structure Constant as a Probe of Chemical Evolution and Asymptotic Giant Branch Nucleosynthesis in Damped Lya Systems," Astrophysical Journal, 615 (2004), pp. 82-97.

101.   Signe Riemer-Sorensen, Steen H. Hansen, and Kristian Pedersen, "Sterile Neutrinos in the Milky Way: Observational Constraints," Astrophysical Journal Letters, 644 (2006), pp. L33-L36.

102.   G. Yamazaki, et al, "Constraints on the Evolution of the Pimordial Magnetic Field from the Small-Scale Cosmic Microwave Background Angular Anisotropy," Astrophysical Journal, 646 (2006), pp. 719-729.

2):

1. R. E. Davies and R. H. Koch, "All the Observed Universe Has Contributed to Life," *Philosophical Transactions of the*

Royal Society of London, Series B, 334 (1991), pp. 391-403.

2. Micheal H. Hart, "Habitable Zones About Main Sequence Stars," *Icarus, 37* (1979), pp. 351-357.

3. William R. Ward, "Comments on the Long-Term Stability of the Earth's Oliquity," *Icarus, 50* (1982), pp. 444-448.

4. Carl D. Murray, "Seasoned Travellers," *Nature, 361* (1993), p. 586-587.

5. Jacques Laskar and P. Robutel, "The Chaotic Obliquity of the Planets," *Nature, 361* (1993), pp. 608-612.

6. Jacques Laskar, F. Joutel, and P. Robutel, "Stabilization of the Earth's Obliquity by the Moon," *Nature, 361* (1993), pp. 615-617.

7. H. E. Newsom and S. R. Taylor, "Geochemical Implications of the Formation of the Moon by a Single Giant Impact," *Nature, 338* (1989), pp. 29-34.

8. W. M. Kaula, "Venus: A Contrast in Evolution to Earth," *Science, 247* (1990), PP. 1191-1196.

9. Robert T. Rood and James S. Trefil, *Are We Alone? The Possibility of Extraterrestrial Civilizations,* (New York: Scribner's Sons, 1983).

10. John D. Barrow and Frank J. Tipler, *The Anthropic Cosmological Principle* (New York: Oxford University Press, 1986), pp. 510-575.

11. Don L. Anderson, "The Earth as a Planet: Paradigms and Paradoxes," *Science, 22 3* (1984), pp. 347-355.

12. I. H. Campbell and S. R. Taylor, "No Water, No Granite—No Oceans, No Continents," *Geophysical Research Letters, 10* (1983), pp. 1061-1064.

13. Brandon Carter, "The Anthropic Principle and Its Implications for Biological Evolution," *Philosophical Transactions of the Royal Society of London, Series A, 310* (1983), pp. 352-363.

14.   Allen H. Hammond, "The Uniqueness of the Earth's Climate," *Science, 187* (1975), p. 245.

15.   Owen B. Toon and Steve Olson, "The Warm Earth," *Science 85, October.*(1985), pp. 50- 57.

16.   George Gale, "The Anthropic Principle," *Scientific American, 245, No. 6* (1981), pp. 154-171.

17.   Hugh Ross, *Genesis One: A Scientific Perspective.* (Pasadena, California: Reasons to Believe, 1983), pp. 6-7.

18.   Ron Cottrell, Ron, *The Remarkable Spaceship Earth.* (Denver, Colorado: Accent Books, 1982).

19.   D. Ter Harr, "On the Origin of the Solar System," *Annual Review of Astronomy and Astrophysics, 5* (1967), pp. 267-278.

20.   George Greenstein, *The Symbiotic Universe.* (New York: William Morrow, 1988), pp. 68-97.

21. John M. Templeton, "God Reveals Himself in the Astronomical and in the Infinitesimal," *Journal of the American Scientific Affiliation, December 1984* (1984), pp. 196-198.

22. Michael H. Hart, "The Evolution of the Atmosphere of the Earth," *Icarus, 33* (1978), pp. 23-39.

23. Tobias Owen, Robert D. Cess, and V. Ramanathan, "Enhanced CO_2 Greenhouse to Compensate for Reduced Solar Luminosity on Early Earth," *Nature, 277* (1979), pp. 640-641.

24. John Gribbin, "The Origin of Life: Earth's Lucky Break," *Science Digest, May 1983* (1983), pp. 36-102.

25. P. J. E. Peebles and Joseph Silk, "A Cosmic Book of Phenomena," *Nature, 346* (1990), pp. 233-239.

26. Michael H. Hart, "Atmospheric Evolution, the Drake Equation, and DNA: Sparse Life in an Infinite Universe," in *Philosophical Cosmology*

and Philosophy, edited by John Leslie, (New York: Macmillan, 1990), pp. 256-266.

27. Stanley L. Jaki, *God and the Cosmologists,* (Washington, DC: Regnery Gateway, 1989), pp. 177-184.

28. R. Monastersky, p. "Speedy Spin Kept Early Earth From Freezing," *Science News, 143* (1993), p. 373.

29. The editors, "Our Friend Jove," *Discover.* (July 1993) p. 15.

30. Jacques Laskar, "Large-Scale Chaos in the Solar System," *Astronomy and Astrophysics, 287* (1994), pp. 109-113.

31. Richard A. Kerr, "The Solar System's New Diversity," *Science, 265* (1994), pp. 1360-1362.

32. Richard A. Kerr, "When Comparative Planetology Hit Its Target," *Science 265* (1994), p. 1361.

33. W. R. Kuhn, J. C. G. Walker, and H. G. Marshall, "The Effect on Earth's

Surface Temperature from Variations in Rotation Rate, Continent Formation, Solar Luminosity, and Carbon Dioxide," *Journal of Geophysical Research, 94* (1989), pp. 11,129-131,136.

34.   Gregory S. Jenkins, Hal G. Marshall, and W. R. Kuhn, "Pre-Cambrian Climate: The Effects of Land Area and Earth's Rotation Rate," *Journal of Geophysical Research, Series D, 98* (1993), pp. 8785-8791.

35.   K. J. Zahnle and J. C. G. Walker, "A Constant Daylength During the Precambrian Era?" *Precambrian Research, 37* (1987), pp. 95-105.

36.   M. J. Newman and R. T. Rood, "Implications of the Solar Evolution for the Earth's Early Atmosphere," *Science, 198* (1977), pages 1035-1037.

37.   J. C. G. Walker and K. J. Zahnle, "Lunar Nodal Tides and Distance to the Moon During the Precambrian," *Nature, 320* (1986), pp. 600-602.

38.   J. F. Kasting and J. B. Pollack, "Effects of High CO_2 Levels on Surface Temperatures and Atmospheric Oxidation State of the Early Earth," *Journal of Atmospheric Chemistry, 1* (1984), pp. 403-428.

39.   H. G. Marshall, J. C. G. Walker, and W. R. Kuhn, "Long Term Climate Change and the Geochemical Cycle of Carbon," *Journal of Geophysical Research, 93* (1988), pp. 791-801.

40.   Pieter G. van Dokkum, et al, "A High Merger Fraction in the Rich Cluster MS 1054-03 at z = 0.83: Direct Evidence for Hierarchical Formation of Massive Galaxies," *Astrophysical Journal Letters, 520* (1999), pp. L95-L98.

41.   Anatoly Klypin, Andrey V. Kravtsov, and Octavio Valenzuela, "Where Are the Missing Galactic Satellites?" *Astrophysical Journal, 522* (1999), pp. 82-92.

42.   Roland Buser, "The Formation and Early Evolution of the Milky Way Galaxy," *Science, 287* (2000), pp. 69-74.

43.   Robert Irion, "A Crushing End for our Galaxy," *Science, 287* (2000), pp. 62-64.

44.   D. M. Murphy, et al, "Influence of Sea Salt on Aerosol Radiative Properties in the Southern Ocean Marine Boundary Layer, *Nature, 392* (1998), pp. 62-65.

45.   Neil F. Comins, *What If The Moon Didn't Exist?* (New York: HarperCollins, 1993), pp.2-8, 53-65.

46.   Hugh Ross, "Lunar Origin Update," *Facts & Faith,* v. 9, n. 1 (1995), pp. 1-3.

47.   Jack J. Lissauer, "It's Not Easy to Make the Moon," *Nature 389* (1997), pp. 327-328.

48.   Sigeru Ida, Robin M. Canup, and Glen R. Stewart, "Lunar Accretion

from an Impact-Generated Disk," *Nature 389* (1997), pp. 353-357.

49.   Louis A. Codispoti, "The Limits to Growth," *Nature 387* (1997), pp. 237.

50.   Kenneth H. Coale, "A Massive PhytoPlankton Bloom Induced by an Ecosystem-Scale Iron Fertilization Experiment in the Equatorial Pacific Ocean," *Nature 383* (1996), pp. 495-499.

51.   P. Jonathan Patchett, "Scum of the Earth After All," *Nature 382* (1996), p. 758.

52.   William R. Ward, "Comments on the Long-Term Stability of the Earth's Oliquity," *Icarus 50* (1982), pp. 444-448.

53.   Carl D. Murray, "Seasoned Travellers," *Nature, 361* (1993), pp. 586-587.

54.   Jacques Laskar and P. Robutel, "The Chaotic Obliquity of the Planets," *Nature, 361* (1993), pp. 608-612.

55.   Jacques Laskar, F. Joutel, and P. Robutel, "Stabilization of the Earth's Obliquity by the Moon," *Nature, 361* (1993), pp. 615-617.

56.   S. H. Rhie, et al, "On Planetary Companions to the MACHO 98-BLG-35 Microlens Star," *Astrophysical Journal, 533* (2000), pp. 378-391.

57.   Ron Cowen, "Less Massive Than Saturn?" *Science News, 157* (2000), pp. 220-222.

58.   Hugh Ross, "Planet Quest—A Recent Success," *Connections,* vol. 2, no. 2 (2000), pp. 1-2.

59.   G. Gonzalez, "Spectroscopic Analyses of the Parent Stars of Extrasolar Planetary Systems," *Astronomy & Astrophysics* 334 (1998): pp. 221-238.

60.   Guillermo Gonzalez, "New Planets Hurt Chances for ETI," *Facts & Faith,* vol. 12, no. 4 (1998), pp. 2-4.

61.   The editors, "The Vacant Interstellar Spaces," *Discover,* April 1996, pp. 18, 21.

62.   Theodore P. Snow and Adolf N. Witt, "The Interstellar Carbon Budget and the Role of Carbon in Dust and Large Molecules," *Science 270* (1995), pp. 1455-1457.

63.   Richard A. Kerr, "Revised Galileo Data Leave Jupiter Mysteriously Dry," *Science, 272* (1996), pp. 814-815.

64.   Adam Burrows and Jonathan Lumine, "Astronomical Questions of Origin and Survival," *Nature 378* (1995), p. 333.

65.   George Wetherill, "How Special Is Jupiter?" *Nature 373* (1995), p. 470.

66.   B. Zuckerman, T. Forveille, and J,. H. Kastner, "Inhibition of Giant-Planet Formation by Rapid Gas Depletion Around Young Stars," *Nature 373* (1995), pp. 494-496.

67.   Hugh Ross, " Our Solar System, the Heavyweight Champion," *Facts & Faith, v. 10, n. 2* (1996), p. 6.

68.   Guillermo Gonzalez, "Solar System Bounces in the Right Range for Life," *Facts & Faith, v. 11, n. 1* (1997), pp. 4-5.

69.   C. R. Brackenridge, "Terrestrial Paleoenvironmental Effects of a Late Quaternary-Age Supernova," *Icarus, vol. 46* (1981), pp. 81-93.

70.   M. A. Ruderman, "Possible Consequences of Nearby Supernova Explosions for Atmospheric Ozone and Terrestrial Life," *Science, vol. 184* (1974), pp. 1079-1081.

71.   G. C. Reid *et al*, "Effects of Intense Stratospheric Ionization Events," Na*ture, vol. 275* (1978), pp. 489-492.

72.   B. Edvardsson *et al*, "The Chemical Evolution of the Galactic Disk. I. Analysis and Results,"

Astronomy & Astrophysics, vol. 275 (1993), pp. 101-152.

73.   J. J. Maltese *et al*, "Periodic Modulation of the Oort Cloud Comet Flux by the Adiabatically Changed Galactic Tide," *Icarus, vol. 116* (1995), pp 255-268.

74.   Paul R. Renne, et al, "Synchrony and Causal Relations Between Permian-Triassic Boundary Crisis and Siberian Flood Volcanism," *Science, 269* (1995), pp. 1413-1416.

75.   Hugh Ross, "Sparks in the Deep Freeze," *Facts & Faith, v. 11, n. 1* (1997), pp. 5-6.

76.   T. R. Gabella and T. Oka, "Detectiion of H_3^+ in Interstellar Space," *Nature, 384* (1996), pp. 334-335.

77.   Hugh Ross, "Let There Be Air," *Facts & Faith, v. 10, n. 3* (1996), pp. 2-3.

78. Davud J. Des Marais, Harold Strauss, Roger E. Summons, and J. M. Hayes, "Carbon Isotope Evidence for the Stepwise Oxidation of the Proterozoic Environment *Nature, 359* (1992), pp. 605-609.

79. Donald E. Canfield and Andreas Teske, "Late Proterozoic Rise in Atmospheric Oxygen Concentration Inferred from Phylogenetic and Sulphur-Isotope Studies," *Nature 382* (1996), pp. 127-132.

80. Alan Cromer, *UnCommon Sense: The Heretical Nature of Science* (New York: Oxford University Press, 1993), pp. 175-176.

81. Hugh Ross, "Drifting Giants Highlights Jupiter's Uniqueness," Facts & Faith, v. 10, n. 4 (1996), p. 4.

82. Hugh Ross, "New Planets Raise Unwarranted Speculation About Life," *Facts & Faith, volume 10, number 1* (1996), pp. 1-3.

83.   Hugh Ross, "Jupiter's Stability," *Facts & Faith, volume 8, number 3* (1994), pp. 1-2.

84.   Christopher Chyba, "Life BeyondMars," *Nature, 382* (1996), p. 577.

85.   E. Skindrad, "Where Is Everybody?" *Science News, 150* (1996), p. 153.

86.   Stephen H. Schneider, *Laboratory Earth: The Planetary Gamble We Can't Afford to Lose* (New York: Basic Books, 1997), pp. 25, 29-30.

87.   Guillermo Gonzalez, "Mini-Comets Write New Chapter in Earth-Science," *Facts & Faith, v. 11, n. 3* (197), pp. 6-7.

88.   Miguel A. Goñi, Kathleen C. Ruttenberg, and Timothy I. Eglinton, "Sources and Contribution of Terrigenous Organic Carbon to Surface Sediments in the Gulf of Mexico," *Nature, 389* (1997), pp. 275-278.

89.   Paul G. Falkowski, "Evolution of the Nitrogen Cycle and Its Influence on the Biological Sequestration of CO_2 in the Ocean," *Nature, 387* (1997), pp. 272-274.

90.   John S. Lewis, *Physics and Chemistry of the Solar System* (San Diego, CA: Academic Press, 1995), pp. 485-492.

91.   Hugh Ross, "Earth Design Update: Ozone Times Three," *Facts & Faith, v. 11, n. 4* (1997), pp. 4-5.

92.   W. L. Chameides, P. S. Kasibhatla, J. Yienger, and H. Levy II, "Growth of Continental-Scale Metro-Agro-Plexes, Regional Ozone Pollution, and World Food Production," *Science, 264* (1994), pp. 74-77.

93.   Paul Crutzen and Mark Lawrence, "Ozone Clouds Over the Atlantic," *Nature, 388* (1997), p. 625.

94.   Paul Crutzen, "Mesospheric Mysteries," *Science, 277* (1997), pp. 1951-1952.

95.   M. E. Summers, et al, "Implications of Satellite OH Observations for Middle Atmospheric H_2O and Ozone," *Science, 277* (1997), pp. 1967-1970.

96.   K. Suhre, et al, "Ozone-Rich Transients in the Upper Equatorial Atlantic Troposphere," *Nature, 388* (1997), pp. 661-663.

97.   L. A. Frank, J. B. Sigwarth, and J. D. Craven, "On the Influx of Small Comets into the Earth's Upper Atmosphere. II. Interpretation," *Geophysical Research Letters, 13* (1986), pp. 307-310.

98.   David Deming, "Extraterrestrial Accretion and Earth's Climate," *Geology,* in press.

99.   T. A. Muller and G. J. MacDonald, "Simultaneous Presence of Orbital Inclination and Eccentricity in Prozy Climate Records from Ocean Drilling Program Site 806," *Geology, 25* (1997), pp. 3-6.

100.   Clare E. Reimers, "Feedback from the Sea Floor," *Nature, 391* (1998), pp. 536-537.

101.   Hilairy E. Hartnett, Richard G. Keil, John I. Hedges, and Allan H. Devol, "Influence of Oxygen Exposure Time on Organic Carbon Preservation in Continental Margin Sediments," *Nature, 391* (1998), pp. 572-574.

102.   Tina Hesman, "Greenhouse Gassed: Carbon Dioxide Spells Indigestion for Food Chains," *Science News, 157* (2000), pp. 200-202.

103.   Claire E. Reimers, "Feedbacks from the Sea Floor," *Nature, 391* (1998), pp. 536-537.

104.   S. Sahijpal, et al, "A Stellar Origin for the Short-Lived Nuclides in the Early Solar System," *Nature, 391* (1998), pp. 559-561.

105.   Stuart Ross Taylor, *Destiny or Chance: Our Solar System and Its Place in the Cosmos* (New York: Cambridge University Press, 1998).

106.   Peter D. Ward and Donald Brownlee, *Rare Earth: Why Complex Life is Uncommon in the Universe* (New York: Springer-Verlag, 2000).

107.   Dean L. Overman, *A Case Against Accident and Self-Organization* (New York: Rowman & Littlefield, 1997), pp. 31-150.

108.   Michael J. Denton, *Nature's Destiny* (New York: The Free Press, 1998), pp. 1-208.

109.   D. N. C. Lin, P. Bodenheimer, and D. C. Richardson, "Orbital Migration of the Planetary Companion of 51 Pegasi to Its Present Location," *Nature, 380* (1996), pp. 606-607.

110.   Stuart J. Weidenschilling and Francesco Mazari, "Gravitational Scattering as a Possible Origin or Giant Planets at Small Stellar Distances," *Nature, 384* (1996), pp. 619-621.

111.   Frederic A. Rasio and Eric B. Ford, "Dynamical Instabilities and the Formation of Extrasolar Planetary

Systems," *Science, 274* (1996), pp. 954-956.

112.   N. Murray, B. Hansen, M. Holman, and S. Tremaine, "Migrating Planets," *Science, 279* (1998), pp. 69-72.

113.   Alister W. Graham, "An Investigation into the Prominence of Spiral Galaxy Bulges," *Astronomical Journal, 121* (2001), pp. 820-840.

114.   Fred C. Adams, "Constraints on the Birth Aggregate of the Solar System, *Icarus* (2001), in press.

115.   G. Bertelli and E. Nasi, "Star Formation History in the Solar Vicinity," *Astronomical Journal, 121* (2001), pp. 1013-1023.

116.   Nigel D. Marsh and Henrik Svensmark, "Low Cloud Properties Influenced by Cosmic Rays," *Physical Review Letters, 85* (2000), pp. 5004-5007.

117.   Gerhard Wagner, et al, "Some Results Relevant to the Discussion of a Possible Link Between Cosmic Rays and the Earth's Climate," *Journal of Geophysical Research, 106* (2001), pp. 3381-3387.

118.   E. Pallé and C. J. Butler, "The Influence of Cosmic Rays on Terrestrial Clouds and Global Warming." *Astronomy & Geophysics, 41* (2000), pp. 4.19-4.22.

119.   B. Gladman and M. J. Duncan, "Fates of Minor Bodies in the Outer Solar System," *Astronomical Journal, 100* (1990), pp. 1680-1693.

120.   S. Alan Stern and Paul R. Weissman, "Rapid Collisional Evolution of Comets During the Formation of the Oort Cloud," *Nature, 409* (2001), pp. 589-591.

121.   Christopher P. McKay and Margarita M. Marinova, "The Physics, Biology, and Environmental Ethics of

Making Mars Habitable," *Astrobiology, 1* (2001), pp. 89-109.

122.   Michael Loewenstein, "The Contribution of Population III to the Enrichment and Preheating of the Intracluster Medium," *Astrophysical Journal, 557* (2001), pp. 573-577.

123.   Takayoshi Nakamura, et al, "Explosive Nucleosynthesis in Hypernovae," *Astrophysical Journal, 555* (2001), pp. 880-899.

124.   Kazuyuki Omukai and Francesco Palla, "On the Formation of Massive Primordial Stars," *Astrophysical Journal Letters, 561* (2001), pp. L55-L58.

125.   Renu Malhotra, Matthew Holman, and Takashi Ito, "Chaos and Stability of the Solar System," Proceedings of the *National Academy of Sciences, 98* (2001), pp. 12342-12343.

126.   Takashi Ito and Kujotaka Tanikawa, "Stability and Instability of

the Terrestrial Protoplanet System and Their Possible Roles in the Final Stage of Planet Formation," *Icarus, 139* (1999), pp. 336-349.

127.   Li-Chin Yeh and Ing-Guey Jiang, "Orbital Evolution of Scattered Planets," *Astrophysical Journal, 561* (2001), pp. 364-371.

128.   M. Massarotti, A. Iovino, and A. Buzzoni, "Dust Absorption and the Cosmic Ultraviolet Flux Density," *Astrophysical Journal Letters, 559* (2001), pp. L105-L108.

129.   Kentaro Nagamine, Masataka Fukugita, Renyue Cen, and Jeremiah P. Ostriker, "Star Formation History and Stellar Metallicity Distribution in a Cold Dark Matter Universe," *Astrophysical Journal, 558* (2001), pp. 497-504.

130.   Revyue Cen, "Why Are There Dwarf Spheroidal Galaxies?" *Astrophysical Journal Letters, 549* (2001), pp. L195-L198.

131.   Martin Elvis, Massimo Marengo, and Margarita Karovska, "Smoking Quasars: A New Source for Cosmic Dust," *Astrophysical Journal Letters, 567* (2002), pp. L107-L110.

132.   N, Massarotti. A. Iovino, and A. Buzzoni, "Dust Absorption and the Cosmic Ultraviolet Flux Density," *Astrophysical Journal Letters, 559* (2001), pp. L105-L108.

133.   James Wookey, J. Michael Kendall, and Guilhem Barruol, "Mid-Mantle Deformation Inferred from Seismic Anistropy," *Nature, 415* (2002), pp. 777-780.

134.   Karen M. Fischer, "flow and Fabric Deep Down," *Nature, 415* (2002), pp. 745-748.

135.   Klaus Regenauer-Lieb, Dave A. Yuen, and Joy Branlund, "The Initiation of Subduction: Criticality by Addition of Water?" *Science, 294* (2001), pp. 578-580.

136.   Leon Barry, George C. Craig, and John Thuburn, "Poleward Heat Transport by the Atmospheric Heat Engine," *Nature, 415* (2002), pp. 774-777.

137.   Akira Kouchi, et al, "Rapid Growth of Asteroids Owing to Very Sticky Interstellar Organic Grains," *Astrophysical Journal Letters, 566* (2002), pp. L121-L124.

138.   Christian J. Bjerrum and Donald E. Canfield, "Ocean Productivity Before About 1.9 Gyr Ago Limited by Phosphorus Adsorption onto Iron Oxides," *Nature, 417* (2002), pp. 159-162.

139.   David E. Harker and Steven J. Desch, "Annealing of Silicate Dust by Nebular Shocks at 10 AU," *Astrophysical Journal Letters, 565* (2002), pp. L109-L112.

140.   Chadwick A. Trujillo, David C. Jewitt, and Jane X. Luu, "Properties of the Trans-Neptunian Belt: Statistics

from the Canada-France-Hawaii Telescope Survey," *Astronomical Journal, 122* (2001), pp. 457-473.

141.   W. A. Dziembowski, P. R. Goode, and J. Schou, "Does the Sun Shrink with Increasing Magnetic Activity?" *Astrophysical Journal, 553* (2001), pp. 897-904.

142.   Anthony Aguirre, et al, "Metal Enrichment of the Intergalactic Medium in Cosmological Simulations," *Astrophysical Journal, 561 (*2001), pp. 521-549.

143.   Ron Cowen, "Cosmic Remodeling: Superwinds Star in Early Universe," *Science News, 161* (2002), p. 244.

144.   Tom Abel, Greg L. Byran, and Michael L. Norman, "The Formation of the First Star in the Universe," *Science, 295* (2002), pp. 93-98.

145.   Robert Irion, "The Quest for Population III," *Science, 295* (2002), pp. 66-67.

146.   Y.-Z. Qian, W. L. W. Sargent, and G. J. Wasserburg, "The Prompt Inventory from Very Massive Stars and Elemental Abundances in Lya Systems," *Astrophysical Journal Letters, 569* (2002), pp. L61-L64.

147.   Kazuyuki Omukai and Francesco Palla, "On the Formation of Massive Primordial Stars," *Astrophysical Journal Letters, 561* (2001), pp. L55-L58.

148.   A. Heger and S. E. Woosley, "The Nucleosynthetic Signature of Population III," *Astrophysical Journal, 567* (2002), pp. 532-543.

149.   Michael Loewenstein, "The Contribution of Population III to the Enrichment and Preheating of the Intracluster Medium," *Astrophysical Journal, 557* (2001), pp. 573-577.

150.   Takayoshi Makamura, et al, "Explosive Nucleosynthesis in Hypernovae," *Astrophysical Journal, 555* (2001), pp. 880-899.

151.   Steve Dawson, et al, "A Galactic Wind at z = 5.190," *Astrophysical Journal, 570* (2002), pp. 92-99.

152.   John E. Norris, et al, "Extremely Metal-Poor Stars. IX. CS 22949-037 and the Role of Hypernovae," *Astrophysical Journal Letters, 569* (2002), pp. L107-110.

153.   Daniel R. Bond, "Electrode-Reducing Microorganisms That Harvest Energy from Marine Sediments," *Science, 295* (2002), pp. 483-485.

154.   E. L. Martin, et al, "Four Brown Dwarfs in the Taurus Star-Forming Region," *Astrophysical Journal Letters, 561* (2001), pp. L195-L198.

155.   Tom Fenchel, "Marine Bugs and Carbon Flow," *Science, 292* (2001), pp. 2444-2445.

156.   Zbigniew S. Kolber, et al, "Contribution of Aerobic Photoheterotrophic Bacteria to the

Carbon Cycle in the Ocean," *Science, 292* (2001), pp. 2492-2495.

157.   Martin J. Rees. "How the Cosmic Dark Age Ended," *Science, 295* (2002), pp. 51-53.

158.   Jay Melosh, "A New Model Moon," *Nature, 412* (2001), pp. 694-695.

159.   Robin M. Canup and Erik Asphaug, "Origin of the Moon in a Giant Impact Near the End of the Earth's Formation," *Nature, 412* (2001), pp. 708-712.

160.   M. Elvis G. Risaliti, and G. Zamorani, "Most Supermassive Black Holes Must Be Rapidly Rotating," *Astrophysical Journal Letters, 565* (2002), pp. L75-L77.

161.   M. Pätzold and H. Rauer, "Where Are the Massive Close-In Extrasolar Planets?" *Astrophysical Journal Letters, 568* (2002), pp. L117-L120.

162.   Shay Zucker and Tsevi Mazeh, "On the Mass-Period Correlation of the Extrasolar Planets," *Astrophysical Journal Letters, 568* (2002), pp. L113-L116.

163.   B. S. Gaudi, et al, "Microlensing Constraints on the Frequency of Jupiter-Mass Companions: Analysis of 5 Years of Planet Photometry," *Astrophysical Journal, 566* (2002), pp. 463-499.

164.   Motohiko Murakami, et al, "Water in Earth's Lower Mantle," *Science, 295* (2002), pp. 1885-1887.

165.   Lee Hartmann, Javier Ballesteros-Paredes, and Edwin A. Bergin, "Rapid Formation of Molecular Clouds and Stars in the Solar Neighborhood," *Astrophysical Journal, 562* (2001), pp. 852-868.

166.   Renyue Cen, "Why Are There Dwarf Spheroidal Galaxies?" *Astrophysical Journal Letters, 549* (2001), pp. L195-L198.

167.   Thilo Kranz, Adrianne Slyz, and Hans-Walter Rix, "Probing for Dark Matter Within Spiral Galaxy Disks," *Astrophysical Journal, 562* (2001), pp. 164-178.

168.   Francesco Gertola, "Putting Galaxies on the Scale," *Science, 295* (2002), pp. 283-284.

169.   David R. Soderblom, Burton F. jones, and Debra Fischer, "Rotational Studies of Late-Type Stars. VII. M34 (NGC 1039) and the Evolution of Angular Momentum and Activity in Young Solar-Type Stars," *Astrophysical Journal, 563* (2001), pp. 334-340.

170.   John Scalo and J. Craig Wheeler, "Astrophysical and Astrobiological Implications of Gamma-Ray Burst Properties," *Astrophysical Journal, 566* (2002), pp. 723-737.

171.   Jan van Paradijs, "From Gamma-Ray Bursts to Supernovae," *Science, 286* (1999), pp. 693-695.

172.   J. S. Bloom, S. R. Kulkarni, and S. G. Djorgovski, "The Observed Offset Distribution of Gamma-Ray Bursts from Their Host Galaxies: A Robust Clue to the Nature of the Progenitors," *Astronomical Journal, 123* (2002), pp. 1111-1148.

173.   Colin D. O'Dowd, et al, "Atmospheric Particles From Organic Vapours," *Nature, 416* (2002), p. 497.

174.   E. W. Cliver and A. G. Ling, "22 Year Patterns in the Relationship of Sunspot Number and Tilt Angle to Cosmic-Ray Intensity," *Astrophysical Journal Letters, 551* (2001), pp. L189-L192.

175.   Kentaro Nagamine, Jeremiah P. Ostriker, and Renyue Cen, "Cosmic Mach Number as a Function of Overdensity and Galaxy Age," *Astrophysical Journal, 553* (2001), pp. 513-527.

176.   John E. Gizis, I. Neill Reid, and Suzanne L. Hawley, "The

Palomar/MSU Nearby Star Spectroscopic Survey. III. Chromospheric Activity, M Dwarf Ages, and the Local Star Formation History," *Astronomical Journal, 123* (2002), pp. 3356-3369.

177.   Jason Pruet, Rebecca Surman, and Gail C. McLaughlin, "On the Contribution of Gamma-Ray Bursts to the Galactic Inventory of Some Intermediate-Mass Nuclei," *Astrophysical Journal Letters, 602* (2004), pp. L101-L104.

178.   V. A. Dogiel , E. Schönfelder, and A. W. Strong, "The Cosmic Ray Luminosity of the Galaxy," *Astrophysical Journal Letters, 572* (2002), pp. L157-L159.

179.   Ken Croswell, *The Alchemy of the Heavens* (New York: Anchor Books, 1995).

180.   John Emsley, *The Elements, third edition* (Oxford, UK: Clarendon Press, 1998), pp. 24, 40, 56, 58, 60, 62, 78,

102, 106, 122, 130, 138, 152, 160, 188, 198, 214, 222, 230.

181.   Ron Cowen, "Celestial Divide," *Science News. 162* (2002), pp. 244-245.

182.   Ron Cowen, "Cosmic Remodeling : Superwinds Star in Early Universe," *Science News, 161* (2002), p. 244.

183.   Jason Tumlinson, Mark L. Giroux, and J. Michael Shull, "Probing the first stars with hydrogen and helium recombination emission," Astrophysical Journal Letters, 550 (2002), pp. L1-L5.

184.   Y.-Z. Qian, W.L.W. Sargent, and G.J. Wasserburg, "The prompt inventory from very massive stars and elemental abundances in Lya systems," *Astrophysical Journal Letters, 569* (2002), pp. L61-L64.

185.   Steve Dawson, Hyron Spinrad, et al., "A Galactic Wind AT z = 5.190," *Astrophysical Journal 570* (2002), pp. 92-99.

186. John E. Norris, Sean G. Ryan, Timothy C. Beers and Wako Aoki and Hiroyasu Ando, "Extremely metal-poor stars. IX. CS 22949-037 and the role of hypernovae," *Astrophysical Journal Letters, 569* (2002), pp. L107-L110.

187. Martin Elvis, Massimo Marengo and Margarita Karovska, "Smoking Quasars: A New Source for Cosmic Dust," *Astrophysical Journal Letters, 567* (2002), pp. L107-L110.

188. Mark G. Lawrence, "Side Effects of Oceanic Iron Fertilization," *Science, 297* (2002), p. 1993.

189. Charles E. Kolb, "Iodine's Air of Importance," *Nature, 417* (2002), pp. 597-598.

190. Colin D. O'Dowd, et al, "Marine Aerosol Formation from Biogenic Iodine Emissions," *Nature, 417* (2002), pp. 632-636.

191. Richard A. Kerr, "Mantle Plumes Both Tall and Short?" *Science, 302* (2003), p. 1643.

192.   Todd A. Thompson, "Magnetic Protoneutron Star Winds and r-Process Nucleosynthesis," *Astrophysical Journal Letters, 585* (2003), pp. L33-L36.

193.   Andrei M. Beloborodov, "Nuclear Composition of Gamma-Ray Burst Fireballs," *Astrophysical Journal, 588* (2003), pp. 9331-944.

194.   Jason Pruet, Rebecca Surman, and Gail C. McLaughlin, "On the Contribution of Gamma-Ray Bursts to the Galactic Inventory of Some Intermediate-Mass Nuclei," *Astrophysical Journal Letters, 602* (2004), pp. L101-L104.

195.   Sydney A. Barnes, "A Connection Between the Morphology of the X-Ray Emission and Rotation for Solar-Type Stars in Open Clusters," *Astrophysical Journal Letters, 586* (2003), pp. L145-L147.

196.   Jonathan Arons, "Magnetars in the Metagalaxy: An Origin of Ultra-

High Energy Cosmic Rays in the Nearby Universe," *Astrophysical Journal, 589* (2003), pp. 871-892.

197.   Shri Kulkarni, "The Missing Link," *Nature, 419* (2002), pp. 121-123.

198.   F. P. Gavriil, V. M. Kaspi, and P. W. Woods, "Magnetar-Like X-Ray Bursts from an Anomalous X-Ray Pulsar," *Nature, 419* (2002), pp. 142-144.

199.   Harold F. Levinson and Alessandro Morbidelli, "The Formation of the Kuiper Belt by the Outward Transport of Bodies During Neptune's Migration," *Nature, 426* (2003), pp. 419-421.

200.   Rosemary A. Mardling and D. N. C. Lin, "Calculating the Tidal, Spin, and Dynamical Evolution of Extrasolar Planetary Systems," *Astrophysical Journal, 573* (2002), pp. 829-844.

201.   Yu N. Mishurov and L. A. Zenina, "Yes, the Sun is Located Near the

Corotation Circle," *Astronomy & Astrophysics, 341* (1999), pp. 81-85.

202.   Guillermo Gonzalez, "Is the Sun Anomalous?" *Astronomy & Geophysics, 40* (1999), pp. 25-30.

203.   J. L. Turner, et al, "An Extragalactic Supernebula Confined by Gravity," *Nature, 423* (2003), pp. 621-623.

204.   Wolf U. Reimold, "Impact Cratering Comes of Age," *Science, 300* (2003), pp. 1889-1890.

205.   Andrey V. Kravtsov, "On the Origin of the Global Schmidt Law of Star Formation," *Astrophysical Journal Letters, 590* (2003), pp. L1-L4.

206.   Keiichi Wada and Aparna Venkatesan, "Feedback from the First Supernovae in Protogalaxies: The Fate of the Generated Metals," *Astrophysical Journal, 591* (2003), pp. 38-42.

207.   Renyue Cen, "The Implications of Wilkinson Microwave Anisotropy Probe Observations for Population III Star Formation Processes," *Astrophysical Journal Letters, 591* (2003), pp. L5-L8.

208.   Renyue Cen, "The Universe Was Reionized Twice," *Astrophysical Journal, 591* (2003), pp. 12-37.

209.   Hans Kepler, Michael Wiedenbeck, and Svyatoslav S. Shcheka, "Carbon Solubility in Olivine and the Mode of Carbon Storage in the Earth's Mantle," *Nature, 424* (2003), pp. 414-416.

210.   Mario G. Abadi, et al, "Simulations of Galaxy Formation in a L Cold Dark Matter Universe. I. Dynamical and Photometric Properties of Simulated Disk Galaxy," *Astrophysical Journal, 591* (2003), pp. 499-514.

211.   K. Pfeilsticker, et al, "Atmospheric Detection of Water

Dimers Via Near-Infrared Absorption," *Science, 300* (2003), pp. 2078-2080.

212.   A. Finoguenov, A. Burkert, and H. Böhringer, "Role of Clusters of Galaxies in the Evolution of the Metal Budget in the Universe," *Astrophysical Journal, 594* (2003), pp. 136-143.

213.   Marc J. Kuchner. "Volatile-Rich Earth-Mass Planets in the Habitable Zone," *Astrophysical Journal Letters, 596* (2003), pp. L105-L108.

214.   KenjiBekki and Warrick J. Couch, "Starbursts from the Strong Compression of Galactic Molecular Clouds Due to the High Pressure of the Intracluster Medium," *Astrophysical Journal Letters, 596* (2003), pp. L13-L16.

215.   S. Chakrabarti, G. Laughlin, and F. H. Shu, "Branch, Spur, and Feather Formation in Spiral Galaxies," *Astrophysical Journal, 596* (2003), pp. 220-239.

216. Edward W. Thommes and Jack J. Lissauer, "Resonant Inclination Excitation of Migrating Giant Planets," *Astrophysical Journal, 597* (2003), pp. 566-580.

217. J. B. Adams, M. E. Mann, and C. M. Ammann, "Proxy Evidence for an El Nino-Like Response to Volcanic Forcing," *Nature, 426* (2003), pp. 274-278.

218. Shanaka de Silva, "Eruptions Linked to El Nino," *Nature, 426* (2003), pp. 239-241.

219. J. S. Seewald, "Organic-Inorganic Interactions in Petroleum-Producing Sedimentary Basins," *Nature, 426* (2003), pp. 327-333.

220. I. M. Head, D. M. Jones, and S. R. Larter, "Biological Activity in the Deep Subsurface and the Origin of Heavy Oil," *Nature, 426* (2003), pp. 344-352.

221. N. White, M. Thompson, and T. Barwise, "Understanding the Thermal Evolution of Deep-Water Continental

Margins, *Nature, 426* (2003), pp. 334-343.

222.	Anthony C. Harris, et al, "Melt Inclusions in Veins: Linking Magmas and Porphyry Cu Deposits," *Science, 302* (2003), pp. 2109-2111.

223.	Jean S. Cline, "How to Concentrate Copper," *Science, 302* (2003), pp. 2075-2076.

224.	Takaya Nozawa, et al, "Dust in the Early Universe: Dust Formation in the Ejecta of Pupulation III Supernovae," *Astrophysical Journal, 598* (2003), PP. 785-803.

225.	Jason Pruet, Rebecca Surman, and Gail C. McLaughlin, "On the Contribution of Gamma-Ray Bursts to the Galactic Inventory of Some Intermediate-Mass Nuclei," *Astrophysical Journal Letters, 602* (2004), pp. L101-L104.

226.	David Stevenson, "Inside History in Depth," *Nature, 428* (2004), pp. 476-477.

3) http://en.wikipedia.org/wiki/Theory_of_everything.

4) Stephen Hawking, A Brief History of Time (New York: Bantam Books, 1988), p. 123.

5) P.C.W. Davies, Other Worlds (London: Dent, 1980), pp. 168, 169.

6) P.C. W. Davies, "The Anthropic Principle", in Particle and Nuclear Physics

7) Paul Davies, The Mind of God (New York: Simon & Shuster, 1992), p. 169.

8) Fred Hoyle, "The Universe: Past and Present Reflections," Engineering and Science (November, 1981), p. 12.

9) Robert Jastrow, "The Astronomer and God", in The Intellectuals Speak Out About God, ed. Roy Abraham Varghese (Chicago: Regenery Gateway, 1984) p. 22.

10) (References:* Roger Penrose, The Emperor's New Mind, 1989; Michael Denton,

Nature's Destiny, The New York: The Free Press, 1998, p. 9).

11) Barber, Matt; www.Townhall.com, Jan 04, 2012.

12) Hoyle, F. 1982. The Universe: Past and Present Reflections. Annual Review of Astronomy and Astrophysics: 20:16.

13) Ellis, G.F.R. 1993. The Anthropic Principle: Laws and Environments. The Anthropic Principle, F. Bertola and U.Curi, ed. New York, Cambridge University Press, p. 30.

14) Schaefer, Henry F., Science and Christianity. P. 71

15) Davies, P. 1988. The Cosmic Blueprint: New Discoveries in Nature's Creative Ability To Order the Universe. New York: Simon and Schuster, p.203.

16) Davies, P. 1984. Superforce: The Search for a Grand Unified Theory of Nature. (New York: Simon & Schuster, 1984), p. 243.

17) Willford, J.N. March 12, 1991. Sizing up the Cosmos: An Astronomers Quest. New York Times, p. B9.

18) Heeren, F. 1995. Show Me God. Wheeling, IL, Searchlight Publications, p. 200.

19) Casti, J.L. 1989. Paradigms Lost. New York, Avon Books, p.482-483.

20) Margenau, H and R.A. Varghese, ed. 1992. Cosmos, Bios, and Theos. La Salle, IL, Open Court, p. 52.

21) Harrison, E. 1985. Masks of the Universe. New York, Collier Books, Macmillan, pp. 252, 263.

22) Heeren, F. 1995. Show Me God. Wheeling, IL, Searchlight Publications, p. 223.

23) Zehavi, I, and A. Dekel. 1999. Evidence for a positive cosmological constant from flows of galaxies and distant supernovae Nature 401: 252-254.

24) Sheler, J. L. and J.M. Schrof, "The Creation", U.S. News & World Report (December 23, 1991):56-64.

25) Mullen, L. 2001. The Three Domains of Life from SpaceDaily.com

26) Schaefer, Henry F., Science and Christianity. P. 49

27) Egnor, Michael; www.evolutionnews.org, article: Would Dr. Arno Penzias, Nobel Laureate in Physics, Be Blacklisted at Iowa State? June 12, 2007.

CHAPTER THREE

1) Eastman and Missler, The Creator Beyond Time and Space, 76-77.

2) Robert Shapiro, Origins -- A Skeptic's Guide to the Creation of Life on Earth, 1986, 128.

3) Francis Crick, Life Itself -- Its Origin and Nature, Futura, 1982.

4) Johnson, Philip, Darwin on Trial, p.111.

5) Darwin, Charles, Origin of Species, Ch. 6, Sixth Edition, 1872.

6) Woodward, Thomas, Darwin Strikes Back, p.142.

7) Richard Lewontin, Billions and billions of demons, The New York Review, p. 31, 9 January 1997.

8) (REPORT, June 1966. "Confession of Professed Atheist," A. Huxley)

9) Christian de Duve, Nobel laureate and organic chemist, "A Guided Tour of the Living Cell".

CHAPTER FOUR

1) Sagan, Carl, "Life" in Encyclopedia Britannica: Macropaedia (1974 ed.), pp. 893-894.

2) Monod, Jacques, "Chance and Necessity: An Essay on the Natural Philosophy of Modern Biology", (1971), Transl. Wainhouse A., Penguin Books: London, 1997, reprint, pp.142-143. Emphasis in original.

3) I. Prigogine, N. Gregair, A. Babbyabtz, Physics Today 25, pp. 23-28

4) Flew, Anthony, Winter 2005 issue of Philosophia Christi (a publication of Biola University, in California).

CHAPTER FIVE

1. http://www.boundless.org/features/ a0000901.html. Copyright © 2004 J. P. Moreland. All rights reserved. International copyright secured.

2. Ibid.

CHAPTER SIX

1. 1)J. L. Mackie, The Miracle of Theism (Oxford: Clarendon Press, 1982), pp. 115, 116.

2. 2) Ibid., p. 117, 118.

3. Michael Ruse, "Evolutionary Theory and Christian Ethics," in The Darwinian Paradigm (London: Routledge, 1989), pp. 262-269.

4. Ibid.

CHAPTER SEVEN

Jacob Kremer, Die OsterevangelienGeschichten um Geschichte (Stuttgart: Katholisches Bibelwerk, 1977), pp. 49, 50.

Van Daalen, D.H., The Real Resurrection, (London, Collins, 1972), p. 41.

Gerd Lüdemann, What Really Happened to Jesus?, trans. John Bowden (Louisville, Kent.: Westminster John Knox Press, 1995), p. 8.

Luke Timothy Johnson, The Real Jesus (San Francisco: Harper San Francisco, 1996), p. 136.

N. T. Wright, "The New Unimproved Jesus," Christianity Today (September 13, 1993), p. 26.

CHAPTER EIGHT

1. http://www.geocities.com/stonerdon/ScienceSpeaks/science_speaks.html#c9, chapter 3.

2. Ibid.

3. http://www.reasons.org/fulfilled-prophecy-evidence-reliability-bible

CHAPTER NINE

1. STURP Final Report. 1981.

2. Ibid.

CHAPTER TEN

1. P. 5.

2. George Ellis, The Times, Friday September 3rd, 2010, p. 8.

3. Ibid.

4. S. Jaki, Cosmos and Creator, Regnery Gateway, Chicago, 1980, p. 5.

5. http://pajamasmedia.com/blog/proving-the-existence-of-god/

6. A Brief History of Time. p. 175.

7. White and Gribbin, Stephen Hawking; A Life in Science, p. 167.

8. As quoted by Dr. Henry Schaefer in The Real Issue, November/December, 1994.

9. Schaefer, Henry, Science and Christianity, p. 59

10. Letter to Max Born, 4 December 1926

11. Schaefer, Henry, Science and Christianity, p. 60

12. Ibid, p. 61

13. Ibid, p. 60

14. A Brief History of Time, New York, Bantam, 1988, p. 141

15. Ibid pp. 134-5

16. Hawking, S.W. and Penrose, R. 1996. The Nature of Space and Time, p. 20

17. Ibid p. 136

18. Ibid p. 180

19. Ibid p. 180

20. Ibid p. 30

21. Ibid pp. 31-32

22. Ibid pp. 42-43

Made in the USA
San Bernardino, CA
03 December 2015